Praise for Karmic Relief

". . . an intriguing deep dive into karma that many readers should find enlightening. Goldberg ultimately breathes new life into an often overused concept by breaking down karma's core principles and applying them to ordinary life." ***—Kirkus Reviews***

"*Karmic Relief* is a wise, inspiring, and beautiful book offering potent medicine for our times. With the clarity and humility that come from a lifetime of dedicated study and practice, Goldberg invites us to embrace the beauty and power that comes from living ethically." **—Miranda Macpherson, author of *The Way of Grace: The Transforming Power of Ego Relaxation***

"For years, this frequently misunderstood topic has been crying out for illumination. Goldberg takes it on with a relaxed, accessible voice that makes his solid scholarship go down easy. He embodies the kind of practical, humane, nondogmatic wisdom that all spiritual teachers would do well to emulate." **—Dean Sluyter, author of *The Dharma Bum's Guide to Western Literature***

"Karma is a law of reality, and Philip Goldberg's *Karmic Relief* is a powerful guide to living with it wisely." **—Rabbi Rami Shapiro, author of *Zen Mind, Jewish Mind***

"This eminently readable book explains a foundational worldview shared throughout nearly all Asian religions. . . . Drawing from his own experience and the wisdom of countless teachers, Goldberg makes this core philosophy easy to understand, and more importantly perhaps, easy to practice. This book is truly a call to right action!" **—Christopher Chapple, Doshi Professor of Indic and Comparative Theology, and director, Master of Arts in Yoga Studies, Loyola Marymount University**

"At last, a concise, friendly book that explains what karma is—and, crucially, what it's *not*. In his usual lucid, practical, and entertaining style, Phil Goldberg gives us everything we need to reset our Karmic Positioning System and glide into a happier future." **—Marci Shimoff, #1 *New York Time* bestselling author of *Happy for No Reason***

"As with his previous book, *American Veda*, Goldberg writes about the ineffable with a master's touch. It is positively thrilling to read an author at the height of his powers. This book is destined to be a classic." **—Stephen Cope, author of *The Great Work of Your Life* and many other books**

"*Karmic Relief* is a gripping, erudite, and immensely practical meditation on the workings of karma and its therapeutic and spiritual value. A must read." **—Swami Medhananda, Vedanta Society of Southern California, Hindu Chaplain at UCLA and USC, author of *Karma and Rebirth in Hinduism***

"Your karma is not your fate—it's your freedom. In *Karmic Relief*, Philip Goldberg hands you the keys to transform your life from the inside out, with timeless wisdom made practical, soulful, and real. Learn how every choice you make can plant seeds of peace, purpose, and joy—for yourself and the world." **—Acharya Shunya, Vedic Scholar and teacher; author of *Sovereign Self***

"Philip Goldberg brings wisdom and discernment to everything he undertakes and every book he writes. This book is no exception." **—Rick Archer, creator and host of "Buddha at the Gas Pump"**

"*Karmic Relief* marries timeless wisdom with modern sensibility, crafting a blueprint for how to co-create a more ethical and compassionate world. With the erudition of a scholar and the warmth of a friend, Goldberg demystifies karma, rendering it both profound and practical." **—Kimberley Lafferty, teacher-practitioner with The Confluence Experience**

"Karma has practically become an English word, yet the depths of this concept are rarely understood in the western world. This book will hopefully go some distance toward correcting this situation." **—Jeffery D. Long, Carl W. Zeigler Professor of Religion, Philosophy, and Asian Studies, Elizabethtown College; author of *Discovering Indian Philosophy***

"Drawing from Eastern traditions while speaking to universal moral insights, Goldberg encourages us to consider how our choices ripple outward—inviting a more thoughtful, grounded, and conscious way of being in the world, especially for a time when quieter wisdom and humane clarity are often drowned by noise and spectacle." **—Father Adam Bucko, director, The Center for Spiritual Imagination, Garden City, NY**

Karmic Relief

Harnessing the Laws of Cause and Effect for a Joyful, Meaningful Life

Philip Goldberg

BOOK PUBLISHING COMPANY
RHINEBECK, NEW YORK

Karmic Relief: Harnessing the Laws of Cause and Effect for a Joyful, Meaningful Life

Paperback ISBN 9781958972991
eBook ISBN 9781966608004

Library of Congress Cataloging-in-Publication Data

Names: Goldberg, Philip, 1944- author
Title: Karmic relief : harnessing the laws of cause-and-effect for a joyful, meaningful life / Philip Goldberg.
Description: Rhinebeck, New York : Monkfish Book Publishing Company, [2025] | Includes bibliographical references.
Identifiers: LCCN 2025019042 (print) | LCCN 2025019043 (ebook) | ISBN 9781958972991 paperback | ISBN 9781966608004 ebook
Subjects: LCSH: Karma | Conduct of life | Happiness
Classification: LCC BL2015.K3 G65 2025 (print) | LCC BL2015.K3 (ebook) | DDC 294.3/422--dc23/eng/20250505
LC record available at https://lccn.loc.gov/2025019042
LC ebook record available at https://lccn.loc.gov/2025019043

Book and cover design by Colin Rolfe

Monkfish Book Publishing Company
22 East Market Street, Suite 304
Rhinebeck, New York 12572
(845) 876-4861
monkfishpublishing.com

To my intuitive wife, Lori, who kept saying,
"I think you should write that book on karma."

Contents

Introduction

Karma has been on my mind for more than half a century. It was one of many concepts I absorbed as a young seeker drawn like an iron filing to the magnet of Eastern philosophy. Hungry for answers to life's Big Questions and desperate for guideposts to a fulfilling existence, I read voraciously about what we call Hinduism and Buddhism and experimented with practices drawn from those traditions. As a kid from the New York streets, I was innately skeptical, and as a counterculture inhabitant, I did not trust authority or take anything on faith. The Eastern precepts I was drawn to seemed profoundly rational; they held up to reason, were endorsed by eminent thinkers, and did not contradict known history or science. And the methods I tried out—primarily from the yogic repertoire of mental, physical, and spiritual disciplines—did what they promised, transforming me in a most welcome manner from the inside out.

In large part, that period of exuberant exploration set the template for my subsequent life and work, which have been marked by an ongoing attempt to integrate East and West, spiritual and material, inner and outer. For quite a while, however, I resisted the theory of karma. The idea that iron-clad laws of cause and effect were at play in the cosmos, and that we invariably reap the consequences of everything we do, like it or not, appealed to me. I wanted to believe the universe was fair and just. I simply didn't see enough evidence. Too many blameless people were suffering and too many miscreants were being handsomely rewarded.

Over time, however, karma grew on me. It began to make intuitive sense. It was compatible with teachings that were objectively verifiable or at least jibed with my own experience. So, I gave the concept the benefit of the doubt. In turn, the likelihood that karma was real came to influence my judgment and my decisions.

At a certain point, I saw the word karma cropping up more and more in the media and in conversations with people who had zero interest in anything spiritual or Eastern. I was intrigued and pleased by this development, but also concerned when the concept was misused and misinterpreted. That's when I started to think about writing a book on the subject.

It sat on the back burner for at least ten years, kept alive by occasional reminders from my longtime agent, the late Lynn Franklin, and my wife, Lori Deutsch, both of whom loved the idea and the title, *Karmic Relief*. Eventually, I included it on a list of potential nonfiction books I sent to my then-new agent, Stephany Evans, and she suggested I work on it next. Who am I to argue with three wise women? It was clearly my karma to write the book that's now in your hands, thanks to the good work of my editor, Jon Sweeney, and his Monkfish colleagues.

In researching and writing the book, I kept two principle goals in mind. One was to clearly explain the concept of karma, which is as nuanced as it is simple, while correcting the many misconceptions about it. The second was to help readers apply the principles of karma in their lives to make wiser decisions and chart a smoother, more harmonious and fulfilling path forward.

We all need karmic relief, and the world needs a karmic reboot that would raise the level of collective morality above its currently dismal state. I sincerely hope the book can make a difference, however modestly, on both levels.

Prologue

Once there was a vicious murderer named Angulimala who terrorized the land, vanquishing everyone who tried to subdue him. Having vowed to kill a thousand people, he kept track of the number by cutting off a finger from each of his victims and adding the digit to a garland strung around his neck. When the count reached 999, he decided to complete the task by killing the very next person he saw.

As it happened, the Buddha was lodged in a nearby monastery. Early that morning, as was the custom for monks, he set out toward the nearest town to collect alms. Along the way, he was warned repeatedly that the brutal, merciless Angulimala was in the vicinity. The Buddha calmly continued on his way.

Soon, Angulimala spotted the unarmed monk on the road. He followed his prey with his sword drawn and ready. Buddha kept walking at his normal pace, yet the killer could never catch up to him, no matter how fast he ran. Finally, exhausted and bewildered, Angulimala shouted, "Stop, monk!"

"I have already stopped," the Buddha replied. "It is you who must stop."

This only heightened Angulimala's confusion. He demanded an explanation.

"I have stopped harming living beings," said the awakened one, "and I have renounced violence. But you continue to kill. You must stop."

In an instant, the frenzy in Angulimala's mind and the rage in his heart were calmed. Gazing into the eyes of the wise renunciate before him, he knew there was another way. He cast aside his weapons and asked the Buddha to take him as a disciple.

Angulimala renounced his violent ways, shaved his head, and donned the robes of the monastic order. Redirecting his energy with exemplary discipline, he advanced rapidly in his mastery of meditation, mindfulness, and compassion.

One day, King Pasenadi learned that the notorious Angulimala was in a nearby forest. He assembled a huge army and tracked down the outlaw only to find him in Buddha's compound. Angulimala thought the karmic debt he'd accrued in his murderous past had finally come due. But Buddha assured the king that the man who had once been a coldblooded murderer had been transformed. When the king was satisfied that this was so, he called off his soldiers.

Angulimala's spiritual progress accelerated, but the seeds of his criminal days continued to bear fruit. Sometimes, when he ventured out to gather alms, people would taunt him and pelt him with stones. Buddha explained that the suffering he had to endure was a pittance compared to the lifetimes of torment that were coming to him before his transformation. "Be patient," he told him. "Continue your practices."

Angulimala did as the master advised and eventually attained liberation. Over the centuries, his story has taught countless seekers that wisdom, virtue, and spiritual discipline can lighten the karmic burden of even the darkest deeds.

1

Cosmic Justice

"Man is always throwing his praise or blame on events, and does not see that he only is real, and the world is his mirror and echo. He imputes the stroke to fortune, which in reality he himself strikes." –*Ralph Waldo Emerson*

The first time I heard the word karma was during the era memorialized in upper case as The Sixties. Someone I knew had been busted for marijuana possession. When I told a friend what had happened, he said, "That's some heavy karma, man." I had no idea what the word meant and was too insecure to ask, but I kind of got the gist.

I soon learned more than the gist from authoritative sources. Cultural dynamics and my own determined seeking led me to explore Eastern philosophy, where I kept bumping into karma. As I explained in the Introduction, the notion that our actions are subject to cause-and-effect laws embedded in the cosmos appealed to me, but in the absence of proof I filed it away as a reasonable hypothesis. It eventually matured into a hunch, and then something close to a conviction.

Not very long ago karma was suitable for conversation only in rarified circles; most people either didn't know what it meant or thought the idea was absurd. Needless to say, things changed rapidly. As yoga studios popped up like coffee shops on every other block; as more and more physicians and therapists recommended meditation and mindfulness for stress reduction; and as core precepts of Eastern philosophy started rolling off the least likely tongues, *karma* became ubiquitous. In my 2010 book, *American Veda,* which chronicled the transmission of Indian spirituality to the United States, I wrote: "The word karma crops up everywhere from scholarly journals to cell phone commercials to entertainment reports to conversations of ordinary people who wouldn't know the Vedas from *Vogue*. In back-to-back issues of *Newsweek*, for instance, cultural icons of different eras used it: Norman Mailer and the rapper 50 Cent (who invoked it to explain why he'd been shot nine times)."

As evidence, I cited an episode of a hugely popular (now largely forgotten) TV show, *Desperate Housewives*, in which one character explains to another why things have gone so badly for them: "It's karma. We've been selfish and greedy, and the universe is telling us to be better people."

Now karma is part of our everyday vocabulary. The concept is frequently invoked in the sports pages, for example, whether the writer is wondering about the bad karma of perpetual losers like the New York Jets or reflecting on the good karma of big-budget winners like the Los Angeles Dodgers. The word comes in handy for political reporters too, like the one who used the catch phrase "karma is a bitch" (the title of a 2018 song by one Scott Thompson) to describe the fate of the Wisconsin governor who narrowly lost his re-election bid and couldn't demand a recount because of a law he himself had backed. It turns up in business publications in reference to the ups and downs of companies and industries. And it flies from the mouths of advice-givers and motivational speakers, like Guy Kawasaki who urges success-driven people to improve their tally on the "karmic scoreboard."

Predictably, karma is now all over social media and is frequently employed by TV pundits and talk show hosts. It also shows up on product names and in commercials. Intel, the financial software giant, purchased a super-costly Super Bowl ad to promote its Credit Karma subsidiary. Companies like Intel do not take either branding or ad buys lightly, so it's safe to assume that associating "karma" with "credit" is considered good for business.

So, presumably, is connecting karma with healing. Unsurprisingly, there's a company called Karma Water whose brands include Karma Energy Water, Karma Probiotic Water, and Karma Wellness Water. Somewhat surprising, though, is Karma Medical, which produces wheelchairs with "karma" emblazoned on the sides. Whether it's to suggest that the need for a wheelchair is a consequence of bad karma or that owning their product is a result of *good* karma, I can't say. But someone thought the word would sell wheelchairs.

Also good for business, apparently, are karma T-shirts. The sayings come in many varieties, including "Enjoy Karma"; "Best karma ever"; "I am going to let karma fix it, because if I fix it, I'm going to jail"; and "It's called karma, and it's pronounced ha-ha-ha."

Why stop at individual products? At karmanow.com you can get help with *all* your shopping. The company claims it "harnesses the power of advanced AI to enhance your shopping experience" and that its "technology predicts the optimal time to make a purchase, ensuring you get the best deal possible."

But it's popular music that may have planted karma into more contemporary minds than any other medium. A search for "karma" on iTunes brings up more than 150 songs, some of which have been recorded by superstars over the span of five decades: John Lennon ("Instant Karma," 1970), Boy George ("Karma Chameleon," 1983), Willie Nelson ("Little Old Fashioned Karma," 1983), Radiohead ("Karma Police," 1997), Black Eyed Peas ("Karma," 1998), Alicia Keys ("Karma," 2003), Taylor Swift ("Karma," 2022), JoJo Siwa ("Karma," 2024).

These cultural references tell us two things: First, karma is embedded in the collective awareness. People who write ad copy, create brand names, produce TV shows, and market song titles know that, at the very least, the average American sees the word karma as shorthand for a system of cosmic justice in which everything we do comes back to us in some form of consequence. Second, the concept is, by and large, incompletely understood and frequently misapplied, as we'll see when we dive into its complexities in the coming chapters.

But before we get to that, some history.

The East-to-West Transmission

Karma filtered into Western soil through various streams over the course of a few hundred years as one of many ideas—or, as some prefer, insights or revelations—born in ancient India. Way back in Grecian times, according to the eminent historian Will Durant, the likes of Pythagoras, Parmenides, and Plato were "influenced by Indian metaphysics," and certain key figures, Alexander the Great among them, made their way to India and interacted with yogis. Trading ships sailed from the Middle East to the Asian subcontinent in biblical days, and scholars say that some of the early Christians had contact with Indian sages. Marco Polo and a host of other explorers and traders made their way to South Asia, often bringing home ideas as well as goods. In the modern era, precepts from the spiritual traditions we call Hinduism and Buddhism began to influence Western thinkers as early as the mid-eighteenth-century, when the French philosopher Voltaire opined that "The Veda was the most precious gift for which the West had ever been indebted to the East."

A number of seminal philosophers in Germany, most of whom were associated with the movement known as Idealism, acknowledged their debt to India. "The study of the Upanishads has been a source of great inspiration and a means of comfort to my soul," wrote Arthur Schopenhauer. "From every sentence of the Upanishads deep, original and sublime thoughts arise, and the whole is pervaded by a high and holy, and earnest spirit." It was in those Upanishads, scholars say, where the theory of karma as we've come to understand it was first articulated.

The exchange between India and Great Britain was the most robust. As the colonial superpower strengthened its grip on the subcontinent, scholars were assigned the task of studying the indigenous religions. The purpose was to make it easier for rulers to subjugate the natives and for missionaries to convert them from what they saw as primitive beliefs to the higher order of Christianity. A funny thing happened, however. In an ironic twist, some of the scholars who rummaged through the Indic storehouse discovered unexpected treasures and signs of spiritual genius.[1] Over time—especially during the so-called Hindu Renaissance[2] of the eighteenth century, when hoary precepts were adapted to the modern era—English translations of Sanskrit texts became more accurate and the commentaries more respectful. One of the enthusiasts, Sir William Jones, established The Asiatic Society in Calcutta (now Kolkata) to further the study of Indian religion and culture. As a result of such efforts, the British philosophers and poets known as the Romantics—William Blake, Samuel Taylor Coleridge, William Wordsworth, et al—incorporated Hindu and Buddhist insights into their work.

Karma would have been among the now-familiar precepts that came to the fore with all this admiring attention.

Light from the East in the USA

Like the morning sun, the light from the East rose slowly in the United States. It appeared on the horizon in the eighteenth century and gathered brightness throughout the nineteenth, especially in New England where learned citizens had made Boston "The Athens of America." Eastern ideas, karma among them, were delivered to Americans by the European Idealists and Romantics, and by home-grown Unitarian missionaries in Calcutta, who found, probably to their surprise, kindred spirits in the Hindu reform movement. Early translations of sacred texts, along with commentaries by the first specialists who would come to be called Indologists, arrived in the bustling port of Boston and found their way onto the bookshelves of spiritual adventurers. One of them was the Reverend William Emerson, who edited *The Monthly Anthology* and founded The Anthology Club to encourage discussion of Eastern philosophy.

The good reverend's son, Ralph Waldo Emerson, was exposed to Indic ideas from an early age, and as a Harvard student his passion for them was ignited. As the eminent scholar of religion, Diana Eck, said of the Sage of Concord: "His work, woven seamlessly and sometimes without attribution with citations from his reading of Hindu and Buddhist scriptures, is a kind of literary testimony to the incipient meeting of East and West."[3] The East shaped a generous portion of Emerson's philosophy, and karma was clearly one of the concepts that took hold. His 1841 essay, "Compensation," can be read as an interpretation of karma in the idiom of mid-nineteenth-century New England. "The dice of God are always loaded," he wrote. "The world looks like a multiplication-table, or a mathematical equation, which, turn it how you will, balances itself." He elaborated: "Cause and effect, means and ends, seed and fruit, cannot be severed; for the effect already blooms in the cause, the end preexists in the means, the fruit in the seed."

Emerson, Henry David Thoreau, and the other Concord Transcendentalists were early adopters of Indic ideas, as was the quintessential American poet, Walt Whitman, and their influence is felt today by every student who reads *Walden* or Emerson's essays or Whitman's *Leaves of Grass*. Their impact was multiplied by the New Thought movement, whose best-known school of thought, Theosophy,[4] expounded the theory of karma and its near cousin, reincarnation, in multilayered detail. Those metaphysical pioneers paved the way for Swami Vivekananda, who stole the show at the 1893 World's Parliament of Religions in Chicago and established the template for the parade of gurus, swamis, roshis, lamas, and other emissaries who were destined to follow in his footsteps. One of Vivekananda's lasting contributions is the series of books on the four classical paths of yoga, one of which is Karma Yoga, the pathway of unselfish action void of attachment to outcome. The opening chapter of that volume, occupying about ten percent of the text, is titled "Karma and Its Effect on Character."

The next of the pre-eminent gurus to attract a large Western following—perhaps the biggest following of all—was Paramahansa Yogananda, who left India in 1920 and spent all but one of his remaining thirty-two years in America. Yogananda's written legacy includes copious references to karma. The index to his translation and commentary on the Bhagavad Gita, for instance, contains nearly a full page of karma references, and the term warrants thirty-one index entries in his iconic memoir, *Autobiography of a Yogi.*[5] Strung together, passages such as this—"The equilibrating law of karma, as expounded in the Hindu scriptures, is that of action and reaction, cause and effect, sowing and reaping"—form a neat summary of karmic theory. (In a fitting cross-cultural boomerang, Yogananda also quotes Emerson's "Compensation.")

Karma was also served up on big platters by the Hindu and Buddhist teachers who were embraced by seekers from the 1960s onward. Maharishi Mahesh Yogi, the most famous guru of the era thanks in large part to his embrace by the Beatles, spoke about karma when asked about it, and he elucidated the concept in two widely-read books, *The Science of Being and Art of Living,* which contains eight full pages on the subject, and his commentary on the Bhagavad Gita, which has thirteen references to it, some quite detailed.

What the ambassadors of Eastern wisdom said in their talks and writings was amplified by a who's who of Western scholars, scientists, psychologists, literary figures, and even clerics. In the 60s, when books, not Google searches, were the currency of ideas, seekers who read the works of public intellectuals such as Aldous Huxley, Joseph Campbell, Huston Smith, and Alan Watts, or works of fiction such as Somerset Maugham's *The Razor's Edge*, Hermann Hesse's *Siddhartha* and *Magister Ludi*, or J.D. Salinger's post-*Catcher in the Rye* output, gobbled up ample servings of Eastern philosophy, including morsels of karma and reincarnation. For example, in Salinger's short story, "Teddy," first published by *The New Yorker* in 1953 and later as the last tale in the mega-selling collection *Nine Stories,* the ten-year-old title character tells a companion that, in the most recent of his previous lives, "I met a lady, and I sort of stopped meditating." As a result of that lapse, he says, he "had to get incarnated in an *Amer*ican body," and "it's very hard to meditate and live a spiritual life in America."[6]

As a result of that cultural history, Yusef Abdus Salaam, one of the exonerated Central Park Five whose execution Donald Trump had publicly demanded, could respond with one word, "Karma," when Trump was indicted by a grand jury, and *Washington Post* columnist Kathleen Parker could write, about Harvey Weinstein's and Bill Cosby's convictions being overturned on appeal, "For now, Weinstein and Cosby got lucky, but karma is patient. Their day will come."

By the time 2022 rolled around, one survey[7] found that 55% of Americans believed in karma. Which raises questions such as: What gap has this foreign concept filled? What need has it satisfied?

Karma's Karma

Ever since the first grieving parent shook her fists at the sky because her child was mauled by a tiger and the kids from the next cave were not, or a pious villager demanded to know why he was visited by misery while his debauched neighbors flourished, human beings have tried to understand why the universe is so unfair, or at least appears to be. As historian Will Durant observed in his epic *The Story of Civilization*, "To explain evil, and to find for men some scheme in which they may accept it, if not with good cheer, then with peace of mind—this is the task that most religions have attempted to fulfill." The corollary task, Durant noted, is to explain why the righteous so often suffer and wrongdoers do not.

People in the global West have agonized over this issue since before the Book of Job dramatized it for the ages. The answers have come in basically two forms. One is secular cynicism; to hard-core atheists and materialists, life is obviously unfair. They see no evidence of anything resembling justice in the cosmos. End of story. Get used to it. The traditional alternative is a faith-driven trust that the universe is governed equitably by a Supreme Being. But the faith-driven perspective inevitably leads to a dead-end that no one has ever been able to reconcile to widespread satisfaction: Why would an all-knowing, all-loving, all-powerful God tolerate evil and the apparently needless suffering of innocents?

That question may have triggered more mind-numbing theological debates, hair-splitting logical labyrinths, and deafening shouting matches than any other religious dispute. The conundrum revolves around three qualities attributed to the Lord of the universe: omnipotence, omniscience, and unqualified goodness. If the cosmos is under the management of a deity who's aware of every fallen sparrow, and is also perfectly benevolent and able to do anything and everything, why would the virtuous suffer misfortune while the greedy, the selfish, the cruel, and the immoral get away with murder? Something has to give: either the Almighty isn't all that mighty, or "all-knowing" doesn't really mean knowing *all*, or the God of love rations that love selectively, perhaps even capriciously.

The dominant religious response to the quandary can be summarized in four words that have been heard in churches, synagogues, and mosques for millennia: "It is God's will." The implication is the same as the lesson taught to Job at the climax of his story: what happened may seem to be unjust in earthly terms, but it was part of the divine plan and therefore must be right and good, even if your feeble human minds cannot fathom how that might be so.

It's an argument for the path of least resistance: take the leap of faith and trust the supreme intelligence that runs the show. That approach has soothed many a troubled soul. But it never satisfied everyone, and certainly not those who insist on logic and evidence. Over time, as the age of science and reason matured, fewer and fewer were willing to make the leap. Some thinkers, including eminent Christians like St. Augustine and Thomas Aquinas, attempted a reconciliation based on an assumption about the psyches of wrongdoers. They proposed that the sinner's very knowledge of his or her sins is, *by itself*, sufficient punishment for having committed those transgressions. Emerson hinted at such a proposition too, suggesting that, even in the apparent absence of accountability, "In some manner there will be a demonstration of the wrong to the understanding" and "this deadly deduction makes square the eternal account."

Surely, self-recrimination is one form of karmic consequence, but shame doesn't seem to burden the wicked quite enough to balance the scales. The argument would not be recommended as consolation for someone who got ripped off by a con man, or the parent of a slain child, or the bleeding victim of a racist assault, or, for that matter, an American in 2025 who was befuddled to the point of distraction over why a just God or a system of natural law would allow a purveyor of hatred and lies to become their President, not once but twice.

Over the centuries, so many excellent minds have grappled with the question of whether the cosmos is fair that the enterprise acquired a name: theodicy. The dictionary defines the term as "defense of God's goodness and omnipotence in view of the existence of evil." The arguments made in the theodicy corner of theology can be so tortured that one scholar I spoke to jokingly called it theo-idiocy. Outside the ivory tower, well-meaning clerics continued, with mixed results, to comfort the afflicted with doctrinal bromides. But, despite popular efforts such as Rabbi Harold Kushner's slim bestseller, *When Bad Things Happen to Good People* (1981), no one has convincingly squared the circle. How can all this misery and injustice be possible in a universe governed by an all-loving and all-knowing Deity?

Meanwhile, in the Indic traditions (Hinduism, Buddhism, Jainism, and Sikhism), Western-style theodicy has largely been absent. As historian Will Durant wrote, "The religion of India mitigates the human tragedy by giving meaning and value to grief and pain." That's because the principles of karma are baked in. And, as we've seen, despite its origins in a nation that for centuries was viewed as a backward land shackled by superstitious idol-worship, karma has shed new light on the Judeo-Christian stalemate because leading thinkers found the theory sufficiently plausible to at least warrant consideration.

For many who sense, or merely hope, that the universe is lawful and fair, karma seems more palatable than a system ruled by a meddlesome and inconsistent deity with whom individuals can bargain for a better deal—what one guru called "shopkeeper religion." In its place, karma offers an impersonal ecology of interconnected energies and entities. "You can't petition karma," said a Buddhist master. "It has no ears or eyes."

Karma can be seen as something akin to a scientific principle, like gravity or thermodynamics, more than as a religious doctrine. The late scholar and President of India, Sarvepalli Radhakrishnan,[8] called karma "the counter-part in the moral world of the physical law of uniformity. It is the law of the conservation of moral energy." If you prefer the wisdom of a schlocky TV show, consider this exchange from an episode of *Glee* in the early 2010s. Two characters are engaged in some heavy teenage reflection. "Do you believe in that thing called karma?" one asks. The other says she does, and offers this explanation: "Well, it's the law of physics, whereby, for example, if you do something to hurt someone, well then the laws of the universe will work against you until you get hurt."

Another reason for karma's appeal is that it posits an educational system instead of a judiciary with an enigmatic legal code. Karma's currency is lessons learned or not learned, curricula mastered or not mastered, assignments met or not met, guidelines followed or not followed. It also supports both equal justice and personal responsibility. What could be more American? Or, ironically, more Christian? It has not gone unnoticed that the theory of karma seems more Christ-like than the draconian magistrate favored by fundamentalists. It was, after all, the New Testament that gave us a metaphor so spot on that Eastern gurus have happily borrowed it when talking about karma: "For whatever a man sows, that he will also reap."

Absence of Evidence v. Evidence of Absence

The fact that an idea is popular and emotionally satisfying doesn't mean it's true. The theory of karma may be analogous to Newton's Third Law of Thermodynamics—for every action there is an equal and opposite reaction—but it lacks empirical proof, and anyone holding out for scientific confirmation is in for a long wait, perhaps a never-ending one. It's hard to imagine the theory ever being captured in a mathematical formulation or validated by rigorous, reliable, repeatable experiments.

To a certain extent, cause-and-effect dynamics can readily be observed in everyday human affairs: get caught driving thirty miles per hour over the speed limit and you pay an expensive penalty; perform a good deed and the recipient is likely to return the kindness. But such obvious examples of what John Lennon called instant karma are contradicted by the endless barrage of actions that don't seem to generate any discernible consequences at all, and especially by the all-too-abundant examples of upstanding souls who suffer and reprobates who thrive. There are simply too many innocents who meet horrible fates and too many liars, crooks, and miscreants who ascend to worldly heights.

On its face, then, any assertion that the universe is fair and balanced is as laughable as the same claim made by a popular cable news channel. To accept karma in the face of all the counter evidence requires the kind of long-term view voiced by singer-songwriter Richard Thompson: Good things happen to bad people, but only for a while.

The absence of proof is compounded by another unproven, and perhaps unprovable, concept that would seem to be a necessary accompaniment: reincarnation. It's hard to make the mathematics of karmic justice add up without factoring in rebirth; too many scoundrels die laughing, never having fully tasted their just deserts, and too many moral exemplars spend their final days in sorrow. Reincarnation resolves the issue by allocating unlimited time to balance the books. As the twentieth-century philosopher Sri Aurobindo said in *Rebirth and Karma,* "It is evident that in one life we do not and cannot labour out and exhaust all the values and powers of that life, but only carry on a past thread, weave out something in the present, prepare infinitely more for the future."[9]

In the Bhagavad Gita's famous metaphor, a soul sheds its current body like a worn-out garment, takes a break to assess things, then dons a fresh new form. It's like returning to school after summer vacation to master a new curriculum, learn the requisite lessons, and pass the necessary tests. In the university of reincarnation, doing well leads to favorable matriculation and failures are treated with rehab and remedial studies. As afterlife systems go, this seems far more equitable than having one measly life determine whether you spend eternity in either paradise or hell—Club Med or fiery furnace, as Norman Mailer, a believer in rebirth, once put it—which would be like sealing a child's fate based solely on their first-grade performance. The system's apparent fairness is no doubt why a surprising number of Americans believe in reincarnation—twenty seven percent according to a 2022 YouGov study.[10] (The same study found that 55% believe in karma, which raises the question: How do those who believe in karma but not reincarnation justify their position?)

A case can be made, however, that developments in science offer conceptual support for karma's plausibility.

Good Vibrations

Nikola Tesla may not actually have been the source of the meme attributed to him, but it demands attention nevertheless: "If you want to find the secrets of the Universe, think in terms of energy, frequency, and vibration."

One reason it's easy to dismiss the theory of karma is that human beings appear to be discreet entities—solid objects separated from one another by empty space. A certain degree of connectedness is obvious, but those occur at isolated times and are mediated through the senses. Make a noise and you connect with everyone who detects the sound waves. Turn on a fan and you connect with everyone touched by the wind. Enter a room and you connect with everyone who sees or hears you. But karma makes sense only if we are *never* separated and are, in fact, inexorably and irrevocably connected in a beginningless and endless chain of being. That this assumed linkage is not seen, heard, or felt by ordinary means doesn't disprove it any more than electrons can be declared nonexistent because our unaided eyes can't see them.

If the universe is made of energy, frequency, and vibration, we are led to places we wouldn't dream of if everything was separate and solid. And in fact science tells us exactly that: everything we experience as a discreet object, whether the book you're holding or the hand that holds it, is a vibrating energy system. The objects our senses perceive are made up of molecules, which are made up of atoms, which are made up of what we call subatomic particles—neutrons, protons, quarks, etc.—that aren't particles at all in the billiard balls and grains of sand sense of the word. Instead, in the great paradox of the scientific age, they're more like energy forms that behave as both particles and waves.

In other words, even what seem to be the most unmoving of material objects, like mountains, are humming, spinning, and vibrating at the subatomic level. Which means that everything in the cosmos is in constant motion despite what our senses tell us. As the legendary physicist Richard Feynman put it, "The world is a dynamic mess of jiggling things." Those jiggles are all connected, and the jiggles from every jiggler in turn jiggles other jiggling things. Interconnectedness, not only among objects in close proximity and ecologically linked life forms, but among subatomic entities separated by incomprehensibly vast distances—what is known as quantum entanglement and Einstein referred to as "spooky action at a distance"—is now a scientific given.

Stepping back even further, today's leading contender for the long-anticipated "theory of everything," which would, if proved, unite the discoveries of relativity theory and quantum mechanics, is string theory (like "particle," "string" might evoke too solid an image, but language fails when physics seeps into metaphysics.) String theory proposes that everything in the universe from quarks to galaxies is comprised of infinitesimally small, one-dimensional vibrating strings. That would make rocks, human bodies, and planets bundles of vibrating energies that our senses perceive as separate concrete objects. It is even said that each pulsating "string" emits a different sound, which would align with the systematic study and use of mantras dating back to the Vedic era.

Physicists bristle, justifiably, when non-scientists take their discoveries too far into the realms of philosophy and spirituality. Nevertheless, it doesn't seem unreasonable to point out that a universe comprised of interconnected vibrations lends a certain amount of plausibility to the theory of karma. It's easier to imagine a cause-and-effect dynamic in individual actions if humans are pulsating energy systems with permeable boundaries and infinite links. This is especially so because, as we'll see, karmic law applies not only to our behavior but also to our thoughts, emotions, intentions, and motivations, all of which might vibrate outward from their points of origin.

The potential of science to offer theoretical support for karma is aided by the growing willingness of neuroscientists, psychologists, and philosophers to entertain the possibility that consciousness is not limited to electrochemical interactions in the brain. Determining exactly how mental activity arises from the activity of neurons has proved to be so elusive that it's been labelled "the hard problem," calling into question the materialist assumption that the stuff in our minds is solely a byproduct of events in the brain. Increasingly, it is postulated that consciousness is *not* manufactured in our skulls but rather exists independently and is assembled and processed in brains, much as sound and light waves are reworked in a television set.

The top candidate in the campaign to remove consciousness from the grip of materialism is called *panpsychism*. One of the leading figures in that effort, Philip Goff, a British philosopher and author of *Galileo's Error: Foundations for a New Science of*

Consciousness, explains: "Panpsychism as defended in contemporary philosophy is the view that consciousness is fundamental and ubiquitous, where to be conscious is simply to have subjective experience of some kind." For panpsychists, everything in existence has some kind of "mentality."

This is more consistent with the schools of thought birthed in India than with those birthed by the so-called Enlightenment in Europe. "Panpsychism is increasingly being taken seriously in both philosophy and science," says Goff, but progress is slow: "The supposition that electrons have some form of consciousness, albeit extremely basic, is still thought by many to be just too crazy to take seriously."[11] In the East, few would think it crazy.

Naturally, the possibility that consciousness exists independent of the human body also lends credence to the reincarnation piece of the puzzle. But it should be noted that reincarnation also has other intriguing empirical support. The Division of Perceptual Studies at the University of Virginia's School of Medicine, Department of Psychiatry and Neurobehavioral Sciences, has been studying "cases of the reincarnation type" (CORT) since the 1960s. Led initially by Dr. Ian Anderson and, after Anderson's death in 2007, by Dr. Jim Tucker, the program's database has accumulated more than two thousand documented CORTs, most of them descriptions by children of what appear to be memories of previous lives. The cases taken most seriously are those that can't be dismissed as childhood imagination because they contain verifiable details such as names and locations.

These evolving developments in science and philosophy lend a degree of plausibility to the notion that the laws of karma are embedded in the cosmic operating system. Still, the chances of finding unequivocal proof remain small. The question is, does it matter?

A Karmic Wager

The fact that you're reading this book suggests that you're either convinced that karma, as described in the venerable texts, is real, or that you have a strong hunch it might be. At the very least, you're open to the possibility. If you're on the fence, here's some food for thought.

First, consider the fact that many millions of people over the course of centuries have taken karma for granted. A skeptic would dismiss that as just another primitive fallacy like a flat earth, or perhaps as a fantasy swallowed by the masses for comfort in a cruel world and promoted by religious leaders to get the great unwashed to behave themselves. We desperately want life to be fair, skeptics would say, so some wise guys invented karma the way others made up heaven and hell. It's hard to argue with such perspectives; if wishful thinking came in plastic bags, the discards would have overwhelmed the planet long ago.

Nevertheless, karma has outlasted a lot of worldviews that rose and fell like the tides, and some of the minds that drew up detailed descriptions of karma have contributed other enduring insights as well, some of which are verifiable. Might those seers have penetrated some aspect of natural law in ways similar to the flashes of intuition that produce fruitful scientific hypotheses?

We are accustomed to lending credence to those we recognize as experts. We don't doubt that there are multiple galaxies in the heavens because astronomers with fancy instruments have told us there are. We accept that two-thirds of the water we drink is made up of something called hydrogen and the remaining third is oxygen, because highly trained people with finely tuned microscopes have said it is so. We also trust many of the musings of those we consider exceptionally intelligent even in the absence of empirical proof.

Should the philosophical and spiritual luminaries who made the case for karma be trusted the same way we trust other experts? Perhaps not to the same degree we rely on the scientific process, but let's acknowledge that yogis, rishis, arhats, and bodhisattvas have proven to be reliable experts in their fields. Their own cultures revere them as gifted individuals who refined the inner, subjective means of acquiring knowledge, thereby opening the doors of perception to greater insight. Perhaps their mental capacities were honed by disciplined introspection, just as science refined its methods with space telescopes and MRIs. For those who have experienced a measure of enhanced mental acuity through contemplative practices, that notion is not that big of a stretch.

Consider too all the ordinary folks for whom the theory of karma is perfectly plausible. Is it possible that they're sensing something mysterious and ineffable but nonetheless real? After all, no lab nerd has ever offered quantifiable proof that love exists, but who doesn't believe it does? And no one has ever proven the existence of a nonmaterial essence called God, or Spirit, or any of its other names, but mystics have testified that they've intuited—in some cases directly perceived—such a presence, and their accounts are remarkably consistent across eras and cultures. In other words, what skeptics might call imaginary or delusional might be something more like attunement.

Maybe that's why the vast majority of stories that endure generation after generation reflect something like karmic law. When the bad guys get their comeuppance and the virtuous are redeemed, an intimate chord resonates in the human psyche, and we cheer. Charles Dickens may never have heard the word karma, but its cause-and-effect dynamic is evident in his every tale, just as it is in Homer and Shakespeare and all the other great storytellers. Might that history be considered a type of evidence, just as the ceaseless outpouring of love songs is evidence of something constant and timeless in the human heart?

Again, it's easy to write off everything I've just proposed as a reflection of our inability to accept that events are random and the universe is unfair. We crave order. We're desperate for justice. But maybe fairness, order, and justice are embedded in the primordial structure of the cosmos and live as archetypes in our psyches. Maybe that's why we feel out of sorts when they appear to be absent, just as we ache when love goes missing and weep at the absence of kindness. Perhaps, in other words, the concept of karma isn't wishful thinking so much as an intuition of a deep truth.

Finally, let's consider what might be called a utilitarian argument for favoring karma over chaos. Blaise Pascal, the seventeenth-century French philosopher, facing squarely the fact that the existence of God could neither be proved nor disproved, famously asked himself which was the better bet: believe or not believe. He made a kind of risk-reward calculation, based on the theology of his time: "Let us weigh the gain and the loss in wagering that God is. Let us estimate these two chances. If you gain, you gain all; if you lose, you lose nothing. Wager, then, without hesitation that He is."

Given the prevailing religious doctrines, what came to be known as Pascal's Wager made eminent sense. If he chose to believe and it turned out that God didn't exist, all he'd have lost is some transient pleasures by foregoing what were regarded as sins, whereas if he chose to act on the basis that God did *not* exist and it turned out that God did, he'd be in hot water.

When it comes to karma, it might make sense to emulate Pascal. Would we not be better people if we believed—indeed, even if we suspected—that everything we do has substantive consequences? If we just might reap what we sow, sowing virtuous seeds is a better risk than planting weeds or poisons, even if it means doing without certain satisfactions. Faced with the choice of being kind or cruel, generous or stingy, loving or hateful, karma points clearly in the direction of goodness.

In other words, saying yes, or even maybe, to karma is a better bet than saying no. We'd be better off if we acted *as if* the laws of karma were operative than to behave as though they were not. And wouldn't the world be a friendlier place if everyone made that bet?

2

Fair and Balanced: What Karma Is and What It's Not

"Karma is the eternal assertion of human freedom. Our thoughts, our words and deeds are the threads of the net which we throw around ourselves."–*Swami Vivekananda*

The word karma derives from the Sanskrit root *kri*, to do. It means action, although some translate it as *work*. Simply put, every action—not just human, but *any* action—is karma, and that is how the word is used in some of India's spiritual and philosophical texts. But karma connotes a great deal more than simply action. We know it today as a complex and nuanced theory of cause and effect with an ethical overlay and profound implications for how we behave in the world.

It wasn't always that way. Either the concept of karma was invented by humans and evolved over time, like musical forms, storytelling, and cuisine, or karma is built into the fabric of the universe and was operative at the dawn of creation, and our perception and understanding evolved over time, as in the sciences. In the latter view, the laws of karma as they apply to human life were apprehended layer upon layer, insight upon insight, discovery upon discovery, just as the laws that govern gravity were detected and fleshed out until one day, voila, we had airplanes and moon landings.

As with most things Indian, the earliest known expressions of karma are found in the Vedas, the most ancient of sacred texts. Scholars disagree about the precise chronology of ancient India, sometimes by a thousand or more years, and it is understood that the Vedas were passed from generation to generation as oral tradition for an unknown period of time, perhaps millennia, prior to being written down. That said, the generally accepted timeframe for the accumulation of writings that constitute the four principal Vedas[12] is 1700 to 900 BCE.

Vedic civilization as a whole was ritual-oriented, and the early Vedic texts consist largely of elaborate and precise descriptions of how offerings were to be made and how mantras were to be chanted for the purpose of influencing deities and natural forces. The principle aims were worldly: safety, food, health, and other essentials for human flourishing. Karma was understood in that context primarily as the proper performance of rituals. But there were also behavioral standards whose purpose was to steer individuals to act in ways that enhanced social and cosmic harmony. Writes scholar of religion Shrinivas Tilak: "The Vedic understanding of karma presupposes that there is a fundamental norm of existence in which all beings and processes participate, each according to its own nature. The relationships between the functions of these individual norms hold together the entire world."[13]

According to scholars, the seeds of what would become the diverse and complex schools of thought comprising Hinduism—and, to a different degree, Buddhism, Jainism, and Sikhism—can be found in the Vedic hymns. That would include the doctrine of karma. Proper performance of prescribed rites with the aim of acquiring specific benefits was, in the view of Swami Prabhavananda in *Spiritual Heritage of India*, "the germ of the law of karma" that would be detailed and expanded by later sages.

In the era known as the Brahmanic period (circa 800-600 BCE by most estimates), reincarnation emerges as part of the prevailing belief system and karma becomes more individualized with the notion that people can ameliorate the impact of their karma and alter its course. The primary method for accomplishing this was expounded in texts called Brahmanas, which consisted of commentaries on the Vedas. Now rituals were to be mediated by priests from the brahmin caste with the aim of winning the favor of deities. It was during this period that caste, which originated as occupational categories (*varnas*) based on individual skills and inclinations, became rigidified as a birth-based hierarchical system with brahmins at the top of the heap as the only ones who could mediate between the human and the divine.

In time, the caste system attracted a determined opposition. About midway through the last millennium before the Common Era, a multi-pronged transformation began to take shape, not unlike the response of Jesus of Nazareth to his fellow rabbis who had stricter interpretations of Torah, or of Martin Luther's revolt against the power of the Catholic priesthood. In the Introduction to his *Historical Dictionary of Hinduism,* scholar of religion Jeffery Long characterizes the development as going from "a series of reflections on the nature of ritual to a grand cosmological vision of the oneness of existence."[14] With that vision came a democratization of spirituality and a concomitant emphasis on individual action with respect to karma and its effects. "A ritual act, or *karma,* which in the early Vedic literature was said to lead to a desired effect if performed well and to its opposite if performed poorly, came to refer to all action," writes Dr. Long. "Karma began to take on a distinctly ethical tone, as referring to any morally good or evil action, along with the inevitable effects of such actions."[15]

The beginning of this period (circa 500-400 BCE) is marked by the earliest of the Upanishads, a collection of sacred literature unprecedented in sophistication and influence. The Upanishads—literally, "sitting down near," so-called because much of the content is in the form of dialogue between gurus and disciples—form the foundation of Vedanta philosophy.[16] The word Vedanta means the end of the Vedas, with "end" signifying the last portion of Vedic literature, the end of the Vedic period, and the culmination, or peak, of the wisdom unveiled by the seers. Like other scholars, Tilak sees the Upanishads as heralding a "shift from a ritually oriented belief system to a more practical and empirically oriented action which also opened a new area of ethics. The reformulation of the karma doctrine with moral implications begins to occur in some of the earliest Upanishadic texts."[17]

This verse from the Brihadaranyaka Upanishad (4:4.5) is often cited as a landmark: "As a man acts, so does he become. A man of good deeds becomes good, a man of evil deeds becomes evil. A man becomes pure through pure deeds, impure through impure deeds." In a similar vein, S. Radhakrishnan's account of the history in his two-volume *Indian Philosophy* states: "To remedy the defects of the old Vedic idea, that redemption from sin could be had by sacrifices to gods, great emphasis is laid on the law of karma. . . . not through sacrifices, but through good deeds does a man become good."[18] It should be noted that experts believe that the doctrine of reincarnation also matured during this period.

The Upanishadic spirit of individual spiritual development, free will, and the realization of one's divine nature through direct, unmediated experience blossomed in different forms, at different times, in different corners of the vast Indian subcontinent. So did the spirit of social equality and the rejection of the brahmin-dominated power structure. Two of the early reform movements became so successful that, centuries later, they were designated distinct religions in themselves.[19] One, led by the sage Mahavira, is known as Jainism. The other, slightly later, was led by Siddhartha Gautama, aka the Buddha, and came to be called Buddhism. Dana Sawyer, a retired professor of religion and author of *The Perennial Philosophy Reloaded,* told me that "renegades like the Buddha were the first to say, 'Nope, anyone can reach liberation with right effort.' This idea, also in Vedanta, that one can transcend the field of action and reaction wasn't in early Hindu traditions. It was a radical notion."

Radhakrishnan puts it this way: "By announcing a religion which proclaimed that each man could gain salvation for himself without the mediation of priests or reference to gods, he [Buddha] would increase the respect for human nature and raise the tone of morality." He adds: "After Buddha did his work, the belief in the permanence and universality of natural law became almost an instinct of the Indian mind."[20]

That instinct can be seen in the later Upanishads such as the Katha and Mundaka, as well as in the subsequent development of Vedanta, in the various bhakti (devotional theism) lineages, in later offshoots such as Tantra, and indeed in all the threads of the diverse fabric of Indic philosophies, sects, lineages, and spiritual methodologies. The differences among the various traditions are huge, and at the same time, their similarities, and even uniformities, are striking. Notably, in the context of this book, the basics of karma and rebirth, and the possibility of liberation from karma's grip, are found in virtually all of them. In time, the concept of karma was also incorporated into medicine and law. It is seen in the early texts of Ayurvedic medicine, and in the Dharmasutras, legal treatises composed between 300 BCE and 100 CE. The latter texts, while clearly committed to the caste structure, recognize the role of individual action in producing and ameliorating the effects of karma.

The dynamics of karma were also portrayed in dramatic terms by the great storytellers of India's past—in the heroic epics, Mahabharata and Ramayana, and in the Puranas, a collection of texts that have been compared to Greek and Roman mythology in that the tales largely center on the actions of deities. "Generally speaking, the epic sages and storytellers take up their respective positions within the philosophical lineage of the Upanishads by accounting for the fashioning of human destiny through the medium of human action (karma)," notes J. Bruce Long in an academic anthology titled *Karma and Rebirth in the Indian Traditions.*[21]

Radhakrishnan echoes that conclusion. The Mahabharata, he writes, "accepts the Upanishad theory that all creatures are bound by karma and are released by wisdom."[22] Tilak cites this Mahabharata passage as an example: "That which is ordained in consequence of one's acts of past life pursues the actor even if he tried to leave it behind. It sleeps when he sleeps and does whatever he does. Like his shadow it rests when he rests, proceeds when he proceeds, and acts when he acts. As a calf recognizes and approaches its parent in the midst of even a thousand cattle, even so the acts of a past life recognize and visit the door in his new life."[23]

In the Puranas, which are thought to have been composed over the course of a thousand years beginning around 250 CE, we find more and more methods by which individuals can modify and overcome the impact of karma. "As the doctrines of Yoga entered the Puranic mainstream, Yoga became another means of deliverance," writes the eminent scholar of Hinduism, Wendy Doniger O'Flaherty, citing a Purana that contains "a long chapter on the way that the practice of Yoga releases people from karma." She adds, "Meditation and renunciation are equally effective as karmic antidotes; and later, as pilgrimage begins to usurp the Brahmin's monopoly on deliverance, the Puranas narrate chapter after chapter of glorifications of shrines ... bathing at any one of which is guaranteed to wipe out all one's past bad karma."[24] It should be noted that when the bhakti traditions began to flourish, devotees in large numbers turned to devotional practices aimed at obtaining karmic boons from the pantheon of Hindu deities.

One sliver of the voluminous Mahabharata (it's about four times as long as the Bible) is the 700-verse Bhagavad Gita, known worldwide as a stand-alone text. Surely the most influential of the East's sacred literature, the Gita is thought to have been composed in the last century BCE or the first century CE.

With its affirmation of freedom of choice, its concise explanations of the principal yogic pathways—one of which is karma yoga, commonly called the yoga of action—and its guidelines for virtuous behavior, the Gita can be seen as a flowering of the post-Vedic emphasis on the personal pursuit of spiritual awakening. In that context, Lord Krishna, representing the voice of divine intelligence, elucidates core principles of karma, rebirth, and the means of transcending karmic cause and effect. The Gita does not entirely negate caste, or varna, but it invokes the concept in the context of *dharma*—the responsibilities and ideal behaviors for members of each occupational category—and not in defense of brahmins as spiritual intermediaries (Arjuna, the Gita's protagonist, is of the *kshatriya,* or warrior, varna). It also decisively elevates individual spiritual development over sacrificial ritual. "To the enlightened seer," it states, "all the Vedas are of no more use than a well where all the land is flooded."[25]

We'll return to the Gita for practical guidance later in the book. We'll also draw from the Yoga Sutras, a collection of aphorisms composed by the sage Patanjali in the same broad historical era but as many as three centuries later. Considered the standard text of classical yoga and increasingly referenced by scholars and yogis in the West, the sutras are as practical as they are pithy. Here is one of its references to karma (chapter 2, verse 12): "A man's latent tendencies have been created by his past thoughts and actions. These tendencies will bear fruits, both in this life and in lives to come."[26]

In the ensuing centuries, the understanding of karma evolved, deepened, and diversified. The dominant traditions, and the various schools of thought *within* the traditions, assumed somewhat different positions on the nuances of karmic theory. They differ, for example, about the agency through which karmic effects are administered, whether through disinterested forces analogous to natural laws or through the will of volitional deities (either an Indic version of a Supreme Being or something akin to a committee of divine beings). They differ too on what takes place between lives, and on exactly what gets reborn, with Hindus favoring the notion of a *jiva*—an individual entity similar to what the West calls a soul—and Buddhists replacing that seemingly permanent structure with an ever-changing stream of thoughts, desires, and other mind stuff that yet retains enough packaging, so to speak, for something relatively consistent (neither the same nor entirely different) to transition from one life to the next. Distinctions were also made regarding the relative weight of external actions as opposed to thoughts, feelings, and motivations, as well as the relative power of different types of action (ritual performance, austerities, ethical behavior, etc.) to restructure an individual's karmic balance sheet.

Delving deeper into the weeds, Hinduism, Buddhism, Jainism, and Sikhism came to different conclusions about how to subdivide karma into categories. Sikhs are minimalists; they describe two types of karma, each defined in relation to *Hukam*, a Punjabi term for divine order or what has also been called the will of God. One type, *sukrit karma*, is in harmony with Hukam; the other, *dukrit karma*, is in opposition to Hukam. By contrast, the maximalist Jains divide karma into eight main classes with a whopping 148 sub-classes. Jainism is also distinct in conceiving of karma in almost materialistic terms. In that tradition, writes Radhakrishnan, "karma is a substantive force, matter in a subtle form. . . . The soul by its commerce with the outer world becomes literally penetrated with the particles of subtle matter."[27]

Buddhist treatises, which can be as rigorously crafted as a Supreme Court decision, describe what might be called types of types, or categories within categories, grouped into three sections: the karmic determinants of rebirth, the karmic impact of various actions, and the amount of time it takes for karmic fruits to ripen.

The divisions of karma most commonly encountered in the West are found in both Hinduism and Buddhism. They are:

- *Sanchita karma*: the sum total of an individual's storehouse of karma accumulated from past action and not yet manifested. It has been compared to a seed that hasn't germinated and is said to determine how one tends to act and react in the present.
- *Prarabdha karma*: that portion of sanchita karma that has begun to germinate and will fructify in the present life. In other words, it consists of reverberations of past actions that are winding their way back to us at varying speeds. It has been compared to a potter's wheel: once set in motion it keeps on spinning until it runs its course.
- *Agami karma*: seeds of karma that are being planted in the present and will bear fruit later in this life or in a future lifetime. (Note that some models call agami karma a different name, *kriyamana karma*, and some use the term kriyamana to designate a fourth category, defined as instant or immediate karma, as in: hit someone and get hit back; smile and be smiled at.)

Sorting out the various typologies of karma is a pursuit best left to academics. What matters here are the points of agreement. The traditions concur on these essentials:

~Karma is a universe-wide system of inexorable cause and effect.
~Every action and thought produces effects that return in kind to their source.
~Individuals are free to choose actions that modify the effects of past karma and produce favorable future karma.
~Tried-and-true guideposts and methods have been developed for accomplishing that practical objective.

The usual adages—"What goes around comes around," "We reap what we sow," or the Buddhist aphorism "Whatever deed I shall do, whether good or evil, I shall become the heir of it"[28]—are sufficient for many people. But for those who want to understand karmic law more deeply and apply that knowledge to promote personal transformation and create a more fulfilling life, additional exploration is required, just as "what goes up must come down" is a convenient placeholder for gravity but not sophisticated enough for designing airplanes. This is especially so because misunderstanding karma can lead to trouble. So, let's look at some of the common misconceptions.

What Karma Is Not

A friend of mine named Lily booked a flight to Florida to see her ailing mother. Due to professional obligations, Lily had to arrange the trip weeks in advance. In the interim, her mother's condition grew worse, and she was hospitalized. Now Lily's forthcoming visit took on added poignancy. Then, two days before her scheduled departure, she came down with Covid-like symptoms and was forced to postpone the trip.

As it turned out, Lily did not have Covid and was back to normal in a matter of days. She booked a new flight for exactly a week after the original date. During that week, her mother faded. Lily was told there was nothing more the doctors could do. She went from hoping to help her mother heal to feeling grateful that she'd be at her mother's bedside when she passed. On the day of her departure, weather conditions caused her flight to be delayed for hours. When she finally landed in Florida, Lily learned that her mother had died while the plane was in the air. She was heartbroken. She felt robbed of the precious opportunity to be with her mother when she breathed her last.

"Is this karma?" she asked me.

It was not the right time for a philosophical discourse, so I replied with a simple "Yes, everything is."

"Was I punished for something I did in the past?" Lily asked. "Or was it my karma to cancel the first trip so I'd be there for my father after Mom died?"

I replied, honestly and succinctly, "I don't know."

Like many people, Lily found value in framing an upsetting or uncanny life event through the lens of karma. However, her questions displayed some all-too-common misconceptions.

Karma is not selective

Lily's first question, "Is this karma?" is like asking "Is this weather?" when it rains. Weather is always happening, on mild days and stormy days, hot days and frigid days. So the proper answer to her question would be, "Of course it is. Whatever takes place in the realm of impermanence and flux, aka the world we inhabit, is, by definition, karma. That's how karma rolls—everywhere, like relativity and gravity."

How could it be otherwise? If the concept has any validity at all, it has to be universal. Every event, whether a monumental upheaval or an insignificant hiccup, is an ingredient in the karmic mixing bowl. It's not like the justice system, where only some criminals get arrested and even fewer are prosecuted. It might seem that way at times, but in the long run karma breeches no exception; it forgets nothing; it doesn't get negligent; it doesn't make mistakes.

"Everything we do, physical or mental, is karma," said Swami Vivekananda, "and it leaves its marks on us." That second part—the mark it leaves—is where our understanding of karma moves from abstract to concrete, from theory to law, from cogitation to application. Knowing that in every moment of life we're tasting the fruits of our past actions and, at the same time, planting the seeds of the future should focus the mind.

Karma is not just about retribution

We tend to invoke karma only when something bad happens, a pattern observable in sitcoms and pop songs as well as everyday usage. Karmic lyrics are mainly of the "You done me wrong, and now you're gonna pay" variety—or, in JoJo Siwa's case, the *singer* done wrong: "Karma's a bitch, I should've known better." Rare is the tune or dialogue that attributes falling in love, say, with good karma. But the law applies to blessings as much as to batterings, as Taylor Swift, at least, understands. She contrasts the karma that's coming (like a bounty hunter) to someone who's misbehaved with images of what karma means to her: the breeze in her hair, a purring cat, a relaxing thought, the boyfriend who's coming home to her.

When we're showered by joys, pleasures, and dreams come true, we seldom stop to ponder the karmic patterns that may have produced them, as we do when we're drenched in misery. But the same cause-effect principles apply across the board; some effects are desirable and others are not. As a character in the Mahabharata says, "Happiness comes due to good actions, suffering results from evil actions. By actions all things are obtained, by inaction, nothing whatsoever is enjoyed. If one's action bore no fruit, then everything would be of no avail."

Karma is not about reward and punishment

When Lily asked if she was being punished for something she'd done in the past, she was demonstrating another common misconception: thinking of positive occurrences as rewards and negative ones as punishments. Given the Judeo-Christian image of God as Supreme Judge, which most of us have internalized to one degree or another, the tendency is not surprising.

It's more accurate, however—and far healthier psychologically—to think of events as the *results*, or *consequences,* of past actions, rather than as prizes for being nice and penalties for being naughty. The language of reward and punishment is more suitable for teaching children, or game shows, or councils authorized to bestow boons for conforming to a prescribed code and to penalize violations. By contrast, "results" and "consequences" resemble the cause-and-effect dynamics described by the sciences.

It can be helpful to think of karma as a system of energy exchange. Like forces acting on objects in the physical realm, our thoughts and deeds emit energy, and the force of that energy produces reactions. Scientists might chafe when hearing such metaphors, but as stated earlier, science has revealed that what we perceive as solid entities are vibrating energies operating in lawful ways. Is it unreasonable to propose that thoughts and actions might operate in a similar fashion? Might Einstein's famous protest that God does not play dice apply to human behavior?

Karma is not determinism or fatalism

Karma places responsibility squarely on our shoulders. We set karmic currents in motion through our thoughts and actions. How we respond when those ripples catch up to us is entirely in our hands, and we alone can create a better karmic future by acting appropriately in the present. All of which is predicated on the premise that human beings have free will.

Which raises the perennial question: Do we really have free will, or do we merely operate under the *illusion* of having free will? Let's agree to let philosophers labor over that conundrum, as they have done forever without coming up with a universally accepted answer. Maybe we're totally and unequivocally free. Maybe everything is predetermined, including the choices we think we're making freely. Maybe the truth is some combination of free will and determinism, as the philosopher Alan Watts concluded: "As determined beings we are free, and ... as free beings we are determined." Or, as Paul Brunton, another British thinker steeped in

Eastern wisdom, put it, "The two factors of dynamic freedom and deterministic fate are always at work in our lives. . . . Freewill versus Fate is an ancient and useless controversy, which is purely artificial and therefore insoluble as it is ordinarily presented."[29]

Another way to think of the free will question is that we all labor with combinations of freedom and constraint that vary from one person to the next and from one situation to the next. We're all familiar with ways that our own psyches and our particular circumstances—and, yes, our karma—can conspire to limit our freedom of choice. To cite the obvious, being hospitalized or imprisoned makes us less free to choose a vacation or a shopping spree than would otherwise be the case. So can psychological conditions, whether depression or obsessive-compulsive disorder. Ditto physical conditions, whether allergies or a broken leg. On a more subtle level, as we'll see, we are all karmically restrained by past impressions embedded in what some call the subconscious and others the recesses of the nervous system. The Indic traditions call these impressions *samskaras* and *vasanas*, and their spiritual methodologies are designed to weaken their grip. So, we could say that as individuals evolve spiritually, they become less determined and more free (more on this in a later chapter).

In an interview on the podcast Buddha at the Gas Pump, Swamini Brahmaprajnananda Saraswati invokes a traditional metaphor of cows being tied to a pole to illustrate these variations on free will. A cow tied to a five-meter rope has less freedom to roam than one tied to a twenty-meter rope, and that cow is more constrained than one on a fifty-meter rope, and so on.[30]

Whatever the ultimate reality may be, we undeniably *perceive* that we're making real choices at every juncture of our lives, and we struggle to make decisions precisely because we feel free to make them. Just as I argued that it's wiser to bet that karma is real than to bet that it's not, it's probably more useful to accept that the feeling of free will reflects reality than to assume it's an illusion. And with our freedom comes responsibility.

Karma is not fixed

Not fixed, but fixable. In an interview, Swami Medhananda, a scholar and monk in a lineage that goes back to the legendary nineteenth-century holy man Sri Ramakrishna, and his chief disciple Swami Vivekananda, referred to "the evolutionary doctrine of karma." He distinguished it from the view that sees karma as a system of rewards and punishments. As an evolutionary force, karma not only allows for learning, growth, and transformation, it might be said to *depend* on them. If karma can be considered purposeful, its purpose is to promote our moral and spiritual growth. As noted earlier, it's more of an educational system than a judicial one: learn the right lessons and you move on to the next level of course work; fail to learn and you repeat the class until you get it right.

Karma teaches us through pleasure and pain, victory and defeat, gain and loss, and the experience of suffering might be the most potent teacher of all. Medhananda said that when Sri Ramakrishna was asked why God permits suffering, he replied, "To create saints."

Consider how much more beneficial it is to think of life's difficulties as a lesson plan—an opportunity to wise up and take the next step in the soul's evolution—instead of as a guilt-inducing punishment. Such a view of karma makes every experience grist for the mill. It gives us incentive to ponder what we can learn from our misfortunes instead of just bemoaning them. Chances are we'll take responsibility and look ahead rather than dwell in blame or self-pity. The learning model also takes the sting out of "sin." In fact, karma resonates nicely with the original meaning of sin, which derives from the Greek *hamartia,* one of whose meanings[31] is "off the mark," as when an archer misses the target. It suggests the need for a course correction as opposed to shame.

One of the elegant ironies of karmic theory is that it gets people thinking about the past and the future, whereas the more practical course would be to focus on the here and now. The karmic mail is inexorable; it will be delivered to our doorsteps without fail. The question is, how do we respond when the delivery comes? Do we ameliorate the impact, or do we compound it? That's another entry point for free will. Maharishi Mahesh Yogi, the guru made famous by The Beatles in 1967, once said, "Suffering in the present is due to weakness in the present, not to previous actions." Similarly, the karmic future is shaped in the present either by weakness and ignorance or by strength and wisdom.

Karma is not just about what we do

The complex mathematics of karma entails more than our outward actions. Every spoken word, every thought, every feeling, and every intention is also factored in. So are circumstances. Say, for instance, you run over a dog with your car. Was it because a) the dog darted in front of you on a dark night, b) you swerved to avoid hitting a group of children, c) you were drunk and gleefully aimed the car at the dog? Different scenarios, same result for the dog, but huge karmic differences for you. To paraphrase the old ditty, it ain't what you do, it's the *why* that you do it.

Also entering the calculus is how we respond when we realize we've done something harmful. Lie? Blame? Apologize? Make amends? Change our behavior from then on? The post-Watergate adage "It's not the crime, it's the cover-up" might apply on the karmic level too.

These and other nuances will be addressed in subsequent chapters because they're of great importance in pursuit of our primary goal: upgrading how we respond to the impact of past karma and creating more favorable karma going forward.

Karma is not an excuse

In spiritual circles, when a mass catastrophe occurs, or someone is battered by an exceptional tragedy, it's common to hear remarks such as "Oh well, it's their karma." When I hear that, my jaw clenches. I'm tempted to say: Well, it may indeed be that person's or that group's karma, but how you respond to it is *your* karma. What do you think will produce more favorable karma, being callous or being compassionate?

Karma does not justify apathy, complacency, or indifference, although it's easy to twist the concept to serve that purpose. It does not cancel the ethical imperatives of empathy and caring. It does not nullify the heartache of seeing victims of cruelty or catastrophe suffer. Surely, if karma is a consistent theory, there must be a difference between the karma of those who perish and those who survive so-called "acts of God" or human evils like mass murder. But what those differences are, and why they exist, is beyond our comprehension, and shrugging off the suffering victims because "it's their karma" is its own form of malice with its own karmic consequences. It's reminiscent of early New England settlers who, when a house was set aflame by lightning, would protect the neighboring homes but let the burning one be consumed. Why? Because the lightning strike was surely God's will and therefore the inhabitants deserved it.

Viewing the miseries and misfortunes of life through the lens of karmic law can alleviate a great deal of handwringing and garment-rending. It helps us face the unbearable with a greater measure of grace and equanimity. It enables us to assume a posture of acceptance. But accepting what karma delivers does not translate to nonchalance or heartlessness. It's all well and good to look at refugees from a war zone, or bodies half-buried beneath rubble, or families weeping at a gravesite, and think that some big karmic I.O.U. has been paid off. But that does not relieve us of the imperative, voiced in every spiritual tradition, to respond to the suffering of others with compassion and lovingkindness. If we happen to be in a position to alleviate any of the suffering but instead don a cloak of detachment, we will bear the consequences.

Such misconceptions about karma have not been uncommon

historically, even in the land whose sages gave us the concept in the first place. "It has spawned a brand of fatalism that has paralyzed vast segments of people," notes contemporary teacher Sadhguru Jaggi Vasudev, "and has been used to validate social injustices and political tyrannies of various kinds." It can be much more convenient to write off inequities than to help alleviate them. But doing nothing is itself a form of action and, presumably, produces karma of its own.

Here's a true story of someone who learned the hard way the karma of carelessly misusing the term karma. Glenn Hoddle managed England's soccer team in the 1998 World Cup. Then, in an interview the following year, he said this about disabled people: "You and I have been physically given two hands and two legs and half-decent brains. Some people have not been born like that for a reason. The karma is working from another lifetime. . . . What you sow, you have to reap." After a public outcry, Hoddle was fired, prompting one wry sports official to say, "If his theory is correct, he is in for real problems in the next life. He will probably be doomed to come back as Glenn Hoddle."

Karma's details are not to be deciphered

The proper response to Lily's questions about the hows and whys of her karma would have been to quote the Bhagavad Gita (4:17): "The course of karma is unfathomable" (other translations: "difficult to know," "impossible to understand," "mysterious," "hard to grasp").

In its essence, karma is as simple and straightforward as "we reap what we sow," but its granular intricacies are beyond human comprehension. Trying to figure out exactly what happened in the past to bring about the present, or work out precisely what will happen in the future as a result of what you're doing now, is a fool's errand. You might trick yourself into thinking you know the answer, but if you're honest you'll see that you've entered a morass of guesswork, speculation, and projection. What happened to Lily wasn't the result of her personal karma alone; it was also her father's karma, and her siblings', and especially her mother's. Add in the airline and its employees and all the other passengers affected by the delay, not to mention whatever is responsible for the weather and all the living beings impacted by it. What mortal could possibly make that calculation?

Making karmic events all the more impenetrable is that the same actions produce different consequences depending on who performs it and the various conditions in play at the time. In his chapter in an academic book on karma, Buddhism expert James P. McDermott gives this example: "A trifling deed done by an individual who is generally unscrupulous in his actions will have different consequences than will a similar deed done by one who is more scrupulous about what he does. Such a deed may drag the former down to a hellish existence; whereas in the case of the latter, it may work itself out entirely in this life. The time at which the fruit of a deed ripens is thus dependent upon the circumstances."[32]

Plus, we don't partake only of the karma we create through our own actions. As we'll explore further in chapter 7, whether group or collective karma is a real thing or merely a useful metaphor is subject to debate. What's indisputable is that each of us is embedded in larger entities—families, communities, nations, associations, institutions, etc.—and our karma is affected by other members of those collectives.

And yet, in circles where karma is taken for granted, it's not uncommon to hear people assert that some misfortune occurred because the victim did such-and-such in the past, e.g., to a robbery victim, "You were probably a thief in a previous life." Such neat cause-and-effect links make for entertaining and, for some listeners, convincing stories. They can also serve the psychological purpose of providing certainty where none exists. But they amount to cavalier conjecture, and they sometimes reek of self-inflation. They simply do not do justice to the immense complexity of karmic patterns. Aldous Huxley expressed this in an elegant understatement in his book, *The Perennial Philosophy*: "Karma exists; but its equivalence of act and award is not always obvious and material."

The same is true of speculation about past lives. I can't count the number of people I've heard claim, sometimes with smug certainty, that they or someone else was so-and-so or a such-and-such in a previous life. More often than not, the purported incarnation was a famous or illustrious one, or at least a terribly dramatic one. You seldom hear about lives spent doing mundane work like farming or shopkeeping. I've personally met two women who claimed to have been Mary Queen of Scots. It might be fun to indulge in such guesswork, and it might alleviate the burden of honest introspection into one's personality traits and behavioral patterns, but most gurus and spiritual lineages consider it a useless distraction. "If you want to know about your past lives, look at your current actions," a teacher once said, adding, "If you want to know about your future lives, look at your current actions."

Exactly why are the details of karma considered unfathomable or impossible to figure out? Consider this passage by author Santosh Krinsky, summarizing the perspective of Sri Aurobindo: "There is a vast intertwined movement of different forms of energies, physical, vital, mental and spiritual, each having their own characteristic power and action, but also impacting one another and creating a new result that represents the force of each line of action, but also takes into account the effect of the interaction. A cause-and-effect relationship exists within this framework, but not in the mechanically simplistic manner that we have tended to ascribe to it.

"This process takes place, not solely on an individual basis, but also for the characteristic action of each species of being, and for the interaction between all life forms and the environment within which they live and act, and the movement of Time in the process of manifestation. We see, not a precise machinery, but a living, breathing Being manifesting through the Oneness of the universal life."[33]

If that doesn't dissuade you from trying to work out the details of karma, here's Maharishi Mahesh Yogi: "Every thought, word or act sets up waves of influence in the atmosphere. These waves travel through space and strike against everything in creation. Wherever they strike they have some effect. The effect of a particular thought on any particular object cannot be known because of the diversity and vast extent of creation. This complexity goes beyond the possibility of comprehension."[34]

The Buddha would have concurred. "In the Ekottara Agama, the Buddha lists four things that can neither be conceived of nor explained," wrote Thich Nhat Hanh. Among those four unknowables, right up there with the origin of the universe, is "the notions of karma and consequence." The Buddhist concept *pratītyasamutpāda*,[35] variously translated as "dependent origination," "dependent arising," and "interdependent co-arising," speaks to the unbreakable interconnectedness and ceaseless interaction of all things gross and subtle, including our thoughts and feelings. Traleg Kyabgon, an author and teacher of Tibetan Buddhism, explains the implications: "As everything is interdependently arisen, we do not have the perspective of a solitary agent performing a variety of actions, but a complex multifaceted individual engaged with many diverse roles, intersecting with a very complex world."[36]

Sorting out human affairs is far more complex than calculating when a falling object will hit the ground, or even determining both the position and velocity of a subatomic particle, which Werner Heisenberg's Uncertainty Principle proved to be impossible. But at least physicists can determine probabilities with reasonable accuracy. Can we?

Think of it this way: if a pebble is dropped into a calm pond, a scientist might accurately predict when the first wave will strike the shoreline and return to the point of origin. But imagine eight or ten pebbles dropped into the same pond at close intervals and with different force. The waves will collide with one another, intermingle, and alter the direction, speed, and amplitude of every single ripple. Good luck tracing the reverberations of a single pebble in that dizzying display of turmoil. Now, extend that image to real life situations: at every moment, thousands or millions of thoughts and actions (pebbles) are dropped into the pond in your corner of the universe along with your own, producing uncountable interactions among crisscrossing energy waves.

Even seemingly straightforward actions can be karmically complicated. Say you lie to a loved one. A simple view of karma suggests that down the road someone will lie to you. But who will do the lying? What kind of lie will it be? When will it come? How consequential will it be? Will its effect on you be exactly equal to the effect of your lie? And who's to say that the energy created by your lie will actually come back to you in the form of another lie, as opposed to a different kind of duplicity? To answer those questions, we would have to calculate not only the impact of your lie on the person you told it to, but also on anyone who might have been indirectly affected. We'd also have to consider the rest of your karmic package, as well as that of the person you lied to. Also weighing in: Did you regret telling the lie? Did you try to rectify the damage? Did you vow to make amends? What kind of karma did your related actions generate? Did they compound the negative karma of lying or reduce it?

Unfathomable.

The limits of human comprehension are often reflected in the stories told in every tradition to impart moral and ethical principles. The storytellers simplify reality in order to drive home messages of right and wrong, hence characters who perform selfish or evil acts are punished in the end and the kind and generous ones are amply rewarded. But some morality tales illustrate the point we're making here about karmic complexity and the constraints on what can be deciphered.

Take, for instance, a Talmudic story that was retold in *The Once and Future King*, T.H. White's novelization of the King Arthur tales. In it, the prophet Elijah returns to earth and embarks on a journey. He and his companion come to the home of a poor couple with meager possessions. The woman and man welcome the strangers, feed them milk and butter from their one cow, and insist that their guests sleep in their bed while the couple hunkers down on the floor.

Elijah and his companion awaken to the sound of weeping. The family's cow had died overnight, leaving them even more impoverished.

The travelers spend the next night in a lavish home whose owner treats them with contempt. He feeds them only water and stale bread, and has them sleep in a barn with the cows. In the morning, Elijah notices that a wall is collapsing and pays a mason to fix it.

The prophet's companion, a learned rabbi, is perplexed. He asks Elijah why the kind, humble couple had to lose their cow while the detestable rich man got to have his wall repaired. Elijah explains that the poor man's wife had been destined to die that night, but because of their kindness God took the cow instead. As for the wall, behind it was a treasure chest the owner didn't know about, and now, because of his heartlessness, he never will.

In his iconic *Autobiography of a Yogi,* Paramahansa Yogananda tells a similar story. Sitting at a campfire with a group of disciples, the legendary yogi, Babaji, suddenly lifts a flaming stick and burns the shoulder of one of the men. Why would he do such a thing? "Would you rather have seen him burned to ashes before your eyes, according to the decree of his past karma?" Babaji asks. He then heals the burn with the touch of his hand. "I have freed you tonight from painful death," he says. "The karmic law has been satisfied through your slight suffering by fire."

Moral: sometimes what we see as punishment is actually karmic debt relief.

Were the events Lily experienced as bad karma a subtle form of good karma? Who knows? Who *can* know? In the end, she and her family, like the rest of us, are left, like Job in the Bible, to humble ourselves before the divine and refrain from trying to solve unsolvable mysteries. To paraphrase Alfred Lord Tennyson's famous ode to soldiers riding into battle:[37] Ours not to reason why, ours but to do our best and respect the results.

Karma is not a prison

We are not entangled in a karmic trap. We are not convicts sentenced by the court of karma. It might feel that way at times, but in fact a generous parole process is built into the system. By adjusting our thoughts and behavior we can reduce the impact of past mistakes, cherish the rewards of our good deeds, and set in motion a better karmic future.

That the details are unfathomable might seem frustrating, but it is really emancipating. It frees us to shift our perspective on the karmic winds that blow our way and readjust our internal KPS (karmic positioning system). Instead of "Woe is me," we are prodded to think "What can I learn from this?" If a behavioral pattern has led repeatedly to the same kind of misery, karma prompts us to ask, "What am I doing to create these problems, and how can I break the habit?"

Pleasure comes and goes; pain comes and goes. Good things happen; bad things happen. We get what we want;, we get what we don't want. But knowing that karma is seldom all good or all bad, that gems might be hidden in the mud and flaws are buried in the gems, makes it easier to maintain a degree of equanimity as the karmic weight shifts from one side of the scale to the other.

The freedom inherent in karmic law extends to liberation from the compulsion to blame fate or other people when things don't go our way. It frees us from the indignity of feeling sorry for ourselves or wallowing in a debilitating victimhood. Understood properly, karma plants us firmly in the present, free of obsession with the past and future. Above all, it frees us to learn and grow.

3

Avert the Danger that Has Not Yet Come

"Your trials did not come to punish you, but to awaken you." –*Paramahansa Yogananda*

The title of this chapter is one way of translating chapter 2, verse 16 of The Yoga Sutras, the collection of aphorisms attributed to the sage Patanjali and widely regarded as the definitive text on Yoga philosophy. Other translations include:

- Pain that has not yet come is avoidable.
- The misery which has not yet come is to be avoided.
- Suffering that has not yet arisen can be prevented.
- This pain is to be warded off, before it has come.

The meaning is plain enough: we can't undo the karma we created in the past; the ship has sailed, the horse is out of the barn, the package is on the truck—add the metaphor of your choice—and we can't step in like a traffic cop to stop the process. In that sense, William Faulkner was right when he famously said, "The past is never dead. It's not even past."

Avoiding the misery that might arise when the past catches up to us entails basically three elements: 1) fortifying our defenses by getting stronger mentally, emotionally, physically, and spiritually, 2) continuously depositing good karma into our account to offset debt payments that might be coming due, and 3) reacting skillfully and wisely when the delivery arrives, thereby reducing its impact.

Radical Acceptance

I recently opened a fortune cookie in a Chinese restaurant and read this: "The first step toward change is awareness. The second step is acceptance." Strictly speaking, that's not a fortune, but as everyday adages go, it's not bad advice. A prerequisite to managing karma is recognizing and accept reality for what it is. We find it hard to do that when life seems unfair or fails to meet our expectations. But if everything is governed by karmic law, whatever happens is not only fair but exactly what we need at that moment. It's part of the lesson plan, even if it feels like one of those surprise tests teachers spring on unprepared students.

Our usual reaction when the karmic crap hits the fan is some combination of limiting the damage; trying to stop things from getting worse; figuring out what caused the problem; attributing blame; wallowing in regret and self-recrimination; hoping things turn out better next time. These are all understandable reactions. But the laws of karma insist on another one: radical acceptance.

The expression "It is what it is" may be an overused cliché, but the message is irrefutable. Whatever is simply and irrefutably is. Wishing it weren't so is a colossal waste of energy. The renowned scholar of mythology and religion, Joseph Campbell, said he learned that lesson from the German philosopher Friedrich Nietzsche. "At a certain moment in his life, the idea came to him of what he called 'the love of your fate,'" Campbell wrote in *Reflections on the Art of Living*. "Whatever your fate is, whatever the hell happens, you say, 'This is what I need.' It may look like a wreck, but go at it as though it were an opportunity, a challenge.

If you bring love to that moment—not discouragement—you will find the strength is there. Any disaster you can survive is an improvement in your character, your stature, and your life. What a privilege!"

Acceptance does not translate to complacency or indifference. It by no means stops us from working hard to curb the impact of whatever happened, or from holding others accountable for contributing to the mess. It does, however, mean curtailing the blame game as quickly as possible and limiting the self-indulgent energy drain of regret. It might also mean limiting the analysis of why things happened the way they did.

It can be fruitful to turn to the past and ask what may have brought you to this moment—or brought this moment to you. Sometimes the cause is obvious. Overslept? Cause: you forgot to set the alarm. Hangover? Cause: you drank too much. In more complex situations—shocks, catastrophes, betrayals, sudden losses, major disappointments—it can be helpful to look back and see if we can identify crucial mistakes or figure out what we may have tossed into the karmic stew to make it toxic. Sober reflection can yield life-changing insights; it's what therapists are paid to help us do.

Identifying patterns, for example, can offer potent insights into what we need to learn and how we need to change. As psychologist and Buddhist teacher Jack Kornfield put it, "Traditionally it is said that if we don't honor our unfinished tasks, our karma will remind us, our unresolved conflicts will rearise; we will be forced to turn toward what we have not faced in ourselves. Put simply, the circumstances of human life will insist on getting our attention."[38]

Think of the close, enduring relationships that bring us the greatest pleasure and also, at times, the greatest pain. Think of the friendships and intimate bonds that start out sublime only to erupt in conflict and end for the same reasons that previous ones did. Repeated actions and reactions are clues. Why do we attract the same kinds of lovers and friends? Why do the same issues keep coming up in different settings with different people?

But it's wise to stick to that which is discoverable and actionable. Acceptance means not only acknowledging the reality of the present moment but yielding to the principle we discussed earlier: the intricacies of karma are ultimately unknowable.

Take, for example, the mysterious relationships whose reasons for being defy rationality. I've known my oldest and closest friend since our first day in college, and I've always been baffled by why we're so close when we're so different. I'm straight, he's gay. I'm a sports nut; he wouldn't know a field goal from a home run. I love books; he can't be bothered. I used to wonder about the karma of the friendship. I speculated about our past-life connections. I asked psychics about it. Then, at one point, I decided to stop the foolish rumination and just enjoy the blessing of friendship and the mysterious karmic bond we obviously have.

Similarly, I and many others have wondered how the hell we ended up in the nuclear families we were born into, as they seem to fit us as poorly as the clothes we wore as teenagers. Karmic theory would say we chose those arrangements as good places to work on this incarnation's curriculum, and that we knew our parents and siblings in previous lives in other configurations. It can be helpful and comforting to believe that you weren't born into your family because of random biological events, especially when the interactions get messy and baffling.

A fine example can be seen in the elegant film *Past Lives*, directed by Celine Song. The tender tale of childhood sweethearts, Nora and Hae Sung, who meet after twenty years apart is ultimately reconciled in a bittersweet way by the Korean concept of *in-yun*. Strictly speaking, the term means providence or fate, but it's used to describe the mystery of relationships over the course of lifetimes. At one point, Nora tells Hae Sung, "If two strangers walk by each other and their clothes brush, there must have been something between them in their past lives." If that's so, imagine the karmic connections between lovers, friends, and family members. Korean Buddhists say that married couples have had 8,000 layers of in-yun in the course of 8,000 lifetimes.

The karmic perspective helps Nora and Hae Sung—and the choked-up audience—accept that they will never know the intimacy their bond would seem to point to. In the same way, it can help all of us reconcile the perplexities of relationship. Isn't that enough? Is it necessary to contemplate who was whom in what location at what time in history? Trying to figure out whether Mom was your sister or brother in Elizabethan England, or if your soul and your sister's soul were in the bodies of soldiers storming the beaches of Normandy, makes no sense unless you have flawless psychic ability, and how many of us have that?

Certainly, it can be useful to take a careful, discerning look backward—only not too far. Accepting that some things are unknowable can be challenging, but it's also transformative. Uncertainty can bring us to our knees, figuratively if not literally.

We're like tourists at NASA watching experts operate the control systems. We're like ordinary listeners watching a maestro conduct a symphony orchestra. We're like chess novices watching grand masters slide pieces around the board while computing five moves ahead. We're like children at a magic show. Watch those kids sometime. They don't try to figure out how the magician put the rabbit in the hat. They just watch in delight. They're OK with the mystery. They enjoy being tricked. We should too, when we stand before the hocus pocus of the vibrating universe.

Humility, reverence, surrender—that's what results when we accept the unknowability of karma. And maybe too, if we're capable of summoning it, a state of childlike awe. The funny thing is, those qualities, in and of themselves, help to ameliorate negative karma. They convert not knowing from a source of frustration into a spiritual practice that draws us closer to the divine.

Radical acceptance also renders us more receptive—better

able to deal with whatever is before us. Struggling to figure out what can't be figured out leads to paralysis. Accepting what is for what it is makes us ready to act, and, as Shakespeare has Hamlet say, "the readiness is all." In the play, Hamlet has some serious karma come his way, and he agonizes over it. He tries to comprehend why certain things happened. He ruminates incessantly over what to do or not do. All of which threatens to drive him mad. Then, as he tells his friend Horatio, he realizes there is "a special providence in the fall of a sparrow" and the timing of the fall can't be predicted by soothsayers and readers of tea leaves, because "we defy augury." Accepting that there are forces at work beyond human control enables Hamlet, at long last, to take action.

Like Hamlet, we can't know the whys and wherefores and what's-to-comes. But the good news is, we don't have to know, any more than I have to know how my computer works in order to write this sentence. We just have to be ready to act in a karmically beneficial manner, preferably in a non-habitual, innovative way that nudges the wheel of karma into a new lane. Radical acceptance brings us closer to the desirable state of being that the poet John Keats called negative capability, which he defined as "being in uncertainties, mysteries, doubts, without any irritable reaching after facts and reason." Keats was advising poets to enter that frame of mind, but in a sense we're all poets, improvising in free verse as karma beats on the bongo drums.

What else does acceptance mean? It means taking responsibility for the karmic debt we somehow accrued, even if what we did to incur the debt is unknowable. It means owning whatever arises without feeling sorry for ourselves. It means not sulking in shame like a child who's being punished or glaring in defiance like a criminal who's being sentenced. It means not wishing that things were different—the very definition of unnecessary suffering.

Above all, it means trusting that the cosmos is, in the final analysis, benign, and that karmic law is fair and just. It would be ideal if that understanding were to lead us to see whatever happens as a blessing—a gift to be treasured. But that might be a bridge too far when we're in pain or muddling through some emotional chaos or pulling out our hair over a practical morass. So how about just welcoming whatever presents itself, however undesirable, as not only a necessary consequence of past actions but also precisely what we need? As Eckhart Tolle put it, "Whatever the present moment contains, accept it as if you have chosen it"—because, in effect, you *have* chosen it, or at the very least produced it.

Like countless others, I've always found this passage from Rainer Maria Rilke's *Letters to a Young Poet* of immense inspiration when radical acceptance is called for: "Be patient toward all that is unsolved in your heart and try to love the questions themselves, like locked rooms and like books that are now written in a very foreign tongue. Do not now seek the answers, which cannot be given you because you would not be able to live them. And the point is, to live everything. Live the questions now. Perhaps you will then gradually, without noticing it, live along some distant day into the answer."[39]

You Can't Always Get What You Want

We tend to forget that karma brings good things as well as bad, since it's human nature to think more about potential perils than the possibility of running into an unexpected joy. But even in the throes of delight, satisfaction, and rapture our choices create new and meaningful karma. When you meet with success of some kind, or you're praised, thanked, or rewarded by others, how do you react? Do you gloat? Brag? Puff up your ego? Act as if it's coming to you? Or do you bow (figuratively or literally) in gratitude? Do you express your appreciation with humility and grace? Do you set your sights on getting more of the same in the future, only bigger and better, or do you look for ways to give back? It's worth reflecting on those questions and taking a good look at ourselves when we receive a happy package of karma.

Meanwhile, our bigger concern is what to do when we slip on a karmic banana peel. That's when we're likely to think, "This is unfair. I don't deserve this!" Which is of far less value than accepting what we've been given as precisely what we need at that moment in our life's journey. Seeing events in that light enables us to treat situations the way students are told to treat required courses, or as youngsters are advised to approach a challenging rite of passage—as a temporary bit of unpleasantness that stands between us and a desirable state of affairs. It creates a platform on which to move forward pragmatically, to with all the grace, skill, intelligence, and determination we can muster.

If everything that happens to us is part of the independent study program we signed up for, even if we can't remember having done so, and if the cosmic curriculum is designed to accelerate our spiritual growth, then hardship must be viewed as an essential component of the soul's evolution. The pain can be compared to the side effect of a healing medication, or an annoying but necessary scab on a wound. Holding challenges in this light can turn us away from self-pity and self-recrimination and toward an inspired, hopeful action plan: accept what is, frame the situation as part of our spiritual lesson plan, learn what needs to be learned, and take wise, skillful action.

"Happiness and misery have an equal share in molding character," wrote Swami Vivekananda, "and in some instances misery is a better teacher than happiness." We're all familiar with that concept. We've heard about highly accomplished people who say their most significant learning grew out of their failures. We've all known people—cancer survivors, to cite a common example—who say they've grown immeasurably because of a devastating illness; some even say that their ordeal was the best thing that ever happened to them. Even Holocaust survivors, most notably the author and psychiatrist Victor Frankl, have testified to having grown spiritually while enduring the most unspeakable horrors.

When he was asked who his greatest teacher was, the Dalai Lama memorably answered, Mao Zedong. Really? The Chinese leader who ordered the invasion of Tibet and forced the Dalai Lama and his people into exile? Yes, him, because the appalling misery he unleashed on the Tibetan people forced the Dalai Lama, according to his own account, to learn about patience and compassion at a depth he might never have penetrated otherwise.

Another well-known figure who sculpted vital lessons out of the rubble of pain is Ram Dass, whose celebrated journey from Harvard professor Richard Alpert to psychedelic renegade to mature spiritual teacher hit an unexpected roadblock in 1997, when he had a stroke. Confined to a wheelchair, with one side of his body virtually useless and his speech impeded, he suffered a crisis of the soul that he said was scarier than the physical one. "The stroke wiped out my faith," he said. But in time he came to see the affliction as "fierce grace." He said the debilitating condition brought to his life greater compassion, authentic humility, an appreciation of silence, and insight into how suffering can be "a steppingstone toward a spiritual goal."

It's not just the celebrated who can profit from using karmic disturbances as a platform for growth. Anyone willing to probe the question "What can I learn from this?" can convert the karma of suffering into the karma of blessing.

Some have proposed that upheavals are indications that we've come quite far in our spiritual development. The idea is that our biggest karmic challenges arise when we're advanced enough to handle them. "[A]ll life is in the nature of an intelligence test," wrote Aldous Huxley in *The Perennial Philosophy*, "and the higher the level of awareness and the greater the potentialities of the creature, the more searchingly difficult will be the questions asked." The payoff, he adds, can be bounteous: "The giving of correct answers is rewarded primarily by spiritual growth and progressive realization of latent potentialities, and secondarily (when circumstances make it possible) by the adding of all the rest to the realized kingdom of God."

Tragedy, loss, calamity—these are shocks to the system. They're slaps in the face. But some slaps, like the one Cher delivered to Nicolas Cage in *Moonstruck* as she shouted, "Snap out of it!" can snap us out of our complacency, smugness, egotism, and false certainties. They're powerful teachers, but only if we're open to learning from them; they're powerful motivators, but only if we're courageous, resilient, and resourceful enough to turn the lessons into actions.

As students in the University of Karma, we define our own learning objectives and determine our own rate of progress, mostly without being conscious of doing so. It is human nature to define our lesson plan in the easiest and most convenient way, perhaps by reinforcing what we already believe or by making an undemanding behavioral adjustment, rather than take on a more challenging transformation. Therefore, we have to ask ourselves, not only what there is to learn but what the best and most fruitful lesson might be.

One of the problems with learning the *wrong* lesson is that it can lead to a repeat of old karmic patterns. We make the same mistakes and reap the same unwanted consequences, whether it's getting fired yet again or finding ourselves in yet another overcooked relationship drama, or some other set of circumstances that seems different on the surface but is carried by the same old undercurrents. Here we go again, one more time, take it from the top, until one day we finally snap out of it, grasp what we need to know, and make the appropriate changes. Then, at long last, we might pass the required exam and matriculate to the next grade.

An acquaintance of mine, a serial entrepreneur with a history of successful ventures and many burned bridges, found himself saddled with a legal mess and a crippled business. By his account he'd been swindled by a devious financier, and the chances of recovering his investment were slight. He was, to put it mildly, enraged. What lessons did he take away from the mess? To quote some of the things he told me, "I should never trust guys like him" (without really defining what "like him" meant). "I have to be more ruthless." "I wasn't aggressive enough." "You have to fight fire with fire. I was too honest." In other words, "No more mister nice guy," as if he was ever a nice guy in the first place.

He wanted to have more of the qualities he thought the super successful, dominant figures in business had. He couldn't see it, but it was obvious that he already had those traits in spades. Maybe, karmically speaking, that was precisely the problem. Maybe the better lesson would have been some combination of these: I need to be less attached to bottom line victories and take on projects I find truly satisfying. I should serve others more and feed my ego less. I ought to focus on shared rewards not just what's in it for me. Maybe if I were more honest and fair myself I'd attract the same from others.

You get the idea. We need to learn practical lessons about how best to navigate specific aspects of our lives, but we also need to consider the lessons that can accrue to our karmic advantage across a wide range of situations, responsibilities, roles, and activities. Here we enter into the territory of values and virtues, and that leads to questions such as: If life is a course of study, what am I majoring in? What will make me a better human being? How can I upgrade desirable qualities such as generosity, kindness, and compassion? What will I regret not changing if I find myself on my death bed tomorrow?

Preventive Medicine

Skillful handling of karmic eruptions is as necessary as taking medicine when disease strikes. But the real key to averting the danger that has not yet come is the equivalent of making lifestyle changes so you heal faster from ailments and prevent illness from cropping up in the first place.

In the previous chapter, I noted that when we incur debt it makes eminently great sense to increase our earnings, invest wisely, and lower our expenses so that, when the debt payment comes due, we're flush. In that way the sting of coughing up the dough is minimal, whereas if we have little or no savings, paying off the debt can be devastating. Making changes in thought, speech, and behavior to accumulate positive karma is analogous to refinancing a mortgage, or renegotiating terms with a lender, or making extra payments on a mortgage to reduce the interest burden. As Paul Brunton put it, "If it be true that we cannot wish our bad karma away, it is equally true that we can balance it with good karma and thus offset its results." Maybe it's even possible to behave so impeccably that a karmic debt is virtually eliminated, like a criminal can be granted early parole for good behavior. (For an example, revisit the story of Angulimala in the Prologue.)

Could Jesus have meant something like that when he said, in the Lord's Prayer, "Forgive us our debts as we forgive our debtors"? Is the act of forgiving an example of good karmic behavior that accomplishes the equivalent of having a debt forgiven?

Playing By the Rules

Now we have to ask: Which actions are most karmically beneficial? In a sense, the answer is simple: Be nice, do good. There you have it, Karma 101. Four words your grandmother might have fed you along with a home baked cookie. Other pithy formulas are offered in both religious and secular contexts, the most familiar of which is the Golden Rule. No matter how you were raised, or what belief system you subscribe to, you know some version of "Do unto others as you would have them do unto you." We think of it as a Christian adage, but anyone who's spent any time in interfaith gatherings knows that variations have been expressed in every religious tradition. Here are some commonly cited examples:

Islam: No one of you is a believer until he desires for his brother that which he desires for himself.

Judaism: What is hateful to you, do not to your fellowmen.

Confucianism: Do not unto others that which you would not have them do unto you.

Buddhism: Hurt not others in ways that you yourself would find hurtful.

Hinduism: This is the sum of duty: Do naught unto others which would cause you pain if done to you.

This is timeless and unsurpassable advice. But if it were sufficient to get human beings to behave themselves, the course of history would have been vastly different. Authentic Golden Rule behavior requires a foundation of virtues such as compassion, empathy, and lovingkindness, and while those qualities are built into the human hardware, they are not always accessible. All too often, obviously, they are superseded by their opposites. Virtue has to be taught and modeled by responsible people, so individuals are empowered to cultivate and express their inherent goodness. At the same time, the opposite tendencies have to be renounced and opposed since one bad deed breeds another. As the adage goes, "Hurt people hurt people."

The obvious fact that human beings need guidance, and perhaps some carrots and sticks, to behave in a wholesome way has led smart, caring people throughout time to construct commandments, precepts, edicts, and codes to tell us what to do and what not to do. Some formulations are as simple as a handful of rules. Others are as extensive and elaborate as a law school curriculum. The Torah, for example, contains 613 *mitzvot*, or commandments; 248 are acts Jews are instructed to do, and 365 are prohibitions (one per day!).

Life is complicated, human beings are flawed, and karma is

nuanced and subject to contingencies, so virtually every injunction has given rise to commentary, analysis, discussion, debate, and occasionally, heated arguments. Don't covet, for example. Sounds simple, but what does it mean in practice? How strongly do you have to want something before it becomes covetous? Is coveting certain things a relatively minor offense while coveting others is disastrous? How obsessed do you have to be before the coveting becomes karmically damaging? What if the coveting stays in your mind and you don't take action on it?

Don't kill? That's as universal an edict as you can find. Nevertheless, history teaches that there are exceptions, most notably self-defense and to prevent harm to the innocent. Religions, knowing they had to offer guidelines for when killing is permissible, or necessary, have developed intricate theses about what constitutes a "just war." Naturally, there are disagreements about those criteria not only among the various traditions but also within them. And real life invariably conjures circumstances that are not clearcut, leading well-meaning people to take opposing positions on whether going to war in this situation or that would be justified. The ferocious arguments over Vietnam and Iraq were not just political, they were religious, with fellow religionists going at it like boxers using words instead of fists.

Even familiar maxims like "Treat thy neighbor as thyself" and "Love thine enemies" are more karmically complicated than they appear to be on the surface. What if you're being nice to your neighbor begrudgingly, because your mother or your pastor told you to? Does that produce the same consequences as doing the same good deed out of genuine compassion, or because you empathize with your neighbor's plight and truly care about their well-being? What if you're being nice to your neighbor only because you think it will get God to forgive your other transgressions, or because you just want to accumulate good karma points? Does calculated, self-serving niceness have the same karmic weight as being kind because your heart is genuinely moved?

As for loving our enemies, a cartoon in *The New Yorker* magazine says it best. A couple is exiting a church along with other congregants after a service. The man says to the woman, "How can I love my enemies when I don't even like my friends?"

Sometimes we have to take baby steps, starting with just not hating our enemy, or having a modicum of sympathy and understanding for our enemy, or maybe even being grateful to our enemy for giving us a reason to self-reflect, learn and grow, as the Dalai Lama did with Mao Zedong. Ram Dass, whom we also mentioned earlier, did something similar during Ronald Reagan's presidency. He was so disturbed by his own hatred of Casper Weinberger, the Secretary of Defense, that he placed a photo of Weinberger on his altar, alongside pictures of his beloved guru and assorted saints. Why? To force himself to see his enemy through the same reverential eyes with which he gazed upon spiritual luminaries. (It is said that Ram Dass later tried the same thing with Donald Trump's picture; no word on whether he succeeded.)

We are forced to conclude that the simplest and most straightforward of prescriptions for favorably tilting the karmic scale are neither simple nor straightforward. That's why spiritual leaders and secular philosophers alike have devised sophisticated ethical formulas. Naturally, they differ in their definitions of virtue and sin, good and evil, and other foundational concepts, and some of their prescriptions are peculiar to specific cultures, eras, and belief systems. But a great deal of agreement can also be identified, along with universal dos and don'ts. Kindness is always good; cruelty is always bad. Hence, a great deal of guidance can be derived from diving into any of the great ethical systems.

That said, in the coming chapters we'll draw mainly from the traditions born in India (principally Hinduism and Buddhism) because their moral and ethical systems were developed with karma in mind—meaning that, for them, the cause-and-effect dynamics of karmic law were foundational.

We'll also take the discussion deeper than the behavioral level and address the elements that underly and determine what we say and do. I refer to our physical, mental, and spiritual condition—or, put another way, our thoughts, feelings, and what might be called our state of consciousness. We'll explore another level of karmic consideration as well: the prospect, common to all Indic systems, of transcending karma and becoming liberated from karmic entanglement altogether. But first we'll look at how we behave in the world and the karmically beneficial choices we're advised to make.

4

Do the Right Thing

"Think well before you act. See that you sow the right seed, so that you will not reap a bitter seed later on." –*Swami Satchidananda*

We're always planting karmic seeds. Everything we do, think, or say is a sown seed. Therefore, the logical extension of "you reap what you sow" is that a key task in life is to choose the right seeds and plant them skillfully, in the right way, at the right time, under the right conditions. If you want to grow apples, you have to plant apple seeds. Planting crabgrass seeds in hopes of seeing apple blossoms is either madness or ignorance. So is doing harmful or unethical things and hoping they'll produce the fulfilling life you wish to enjoy in the future. The question arises, then: Which actions give rise to desirable karma, and which produce the opposite? On the one hand, it's so simple we don't need book chapters like this one. As the Dalai Lama was reputed to have said, "No need for temples. No need for complicated philosophy. Your own mind, your heart is the temple. Your philosophy is simple kindness."

On the other hand, it's good to keep in mind that life gets complicated and knowing what the right thing to do is not always straightforward. Most readers of this book are familiar with the dos and don'ts of Western religion and secular culture. So, let's turn to the traditions whose behavioral codes were framed by the principles of karma and see what they have to say.

First, something to keep in mind throughout. We affix labels like Hinduism and Buddhism to the spiritual traditions born in India. We categorize them as religions. But the category "religion" is a Western invention, a vestige of colonialism. As a result, what we typically mean by religion is framed by concepts that don't always fit the spirituality that evolved in the East. That applies not only to areas such as metaphysics, theology, and praxis, but also to ethics. By and large, the Eastern behavioral precepts we'll examine are not the same as commandments, decrees, rules, or religious laws. They're more like instructions for self-improvement. They're considered beneficial to spiritual development and overall well-being, on both the individual and communal levels. That's one reason many Western seekers have found them more palatable than strict mandates from on high that fail to account for human differences and social complexity, and much more acceptable than directives that threaten the non-compliant with draconian punishment. Eternal damnation? No thanks.

So, as we move forward, you will find it most productive to think of the principles we discuss as guidelines or recommendations for creating the most favorable karmic outcomes. "The discipline of karma is purifying and remedial," wrote Radhakrishnan. "Its operation is the energizing of a vital law. It is the business of man to so order his life as to bring it into harmony with this law."[40]

The To-Do List

In The Yoga Sutras, Patanjali describes eight limbs of yoga. The eight components have sometimes been described as steps, implying that each one as to be mastered before the aspirant moves on to the next step in the sequence. But when you think about it, that would be rather impossible. One could spend a lifetime on any of them and never fully master it, since development in certain areas can never be regarded as complete. The term limbs, on the other hand, suggests that the eight function synergistically, with progress in one complementing progress in the others, like pulling one leg of a table simultaneously moves the other legs, and the table as a whole.

That said, the first two limbs consist of behavioral precepts known as the yamas and the niyamas. The yamas are things it's best to refrain from doing; the niyamas are observances, or things we're advised to do. Because there are five of each, the combination is sometimes referred to as the Ten Commandments of Hinduism. This is a misperception since, as noted earlier, they're more akin to spiritual direction than religious mandates. In addition to enhancing social cohesion and harmonious relations, the yamas and niyamas, like all yogic practices, aim to move individuals closer to the state of unified consciousness—aka liberation, awakening, enlightenment—that is the very definition of Yoga in the highest sense. Acting in accord with the yamas and niyamas creates conditions for what we in the West call grace and, as a consequence, augmenting the asset column on the karmic balance sheet.

For reasons known only to Patanjali, the yamas—what we might call "don'ts"—come first. But, since we're conditioned by the phrase "dos and don'ts" to think in that order, we'll reverse Patanjali and begin with the five niyamas: saucha, santosha, tapas, svadhyaya, and ishvara pranidhana. Like most products that come to us in an unfamiliar language from a foreign culture, they require translation, interpretation, and discerning strategies for applying them to our lives.

Saucha

Usually translated as purity, saucha resonates with the proverb "Cleanliness is next to godliness." On the most obvious level, saucha advises us to avoid intoxicants, stimulants, toxins, impure food, polluted air, and other contaminants. But the intent is not just to maintain bodily purity. We're advised to keep our minds and hearts pure as well, by favoring positive thoughts and feelings and taking in only that which elevates, uplifts, and illuminates. In their commentary on the Yoga Sutras, Swami Prabhavananda and Christopher Isherwood use the term "mental diet." "We must regulate our reading, our conversation, and indeed, our whole intake of mental 'food,'" they write, and to "cultivate the society of those who are spiritually minded." Notably, they balance that advice by counseling against extremism. Saucha, they contend, doesn't entail the complete avoidance of light entertainment, or of topics considered worldly or sinful. Puritanical fanaticism, they warn, can "lead to self-righteous pride and a furtive desire for what was forbidden." In addition, they point out that any experience, thought pattern, or topic of conversation can be elevated to a higher, purer level. That's especially true, I would note, when profane subjects are shaped by the hands of a gifted artist.

Commentators agree that the precept counsels not only the clearing of toxins from the body, but the cleansing of toxic thoughts from the mind and toxic emotions from the heart. Further, we are directed to eliminate deeply embedded imprints from past experiences that have lodged in the recesses of the mind-body system. These subterranean impressions, known as vasanas and samskaras,[41] condition how we respond to events, giving rise to either right action or karmically harmful tendencies such as habitual anger, vindictiveness, cruelty, and arrogance. This is similar to what we in the West have come to understand about the enduring impact of trauma and subconscious patterns. The yogic traditions offer methods for cleansing those deep impurities, the payoff of which was expressed most memorably by William Blake: "If the doors of perception were cleansed, every thing would appear to man as it is, Infinite."

We'll consider practical methods of purification in a later chapter. Here, in the context of doing the right thing, two aspects of saucha should be kept in mind: 1) behaving in a pure manner, morally and ethically, is karmically advantageous, and 2) we are more likely to do so if our minds, hearts, and bodies are, relatively speaking, pure.

Santosha

Almost always translated as contentment, santosha might seem out of place in a discussion of behavioral precepts. But it's safe to conclude that the sages had something foundational in mind: cultivating a contented state of being as a precursor to proper speech and action. Contentment suggests psychic balance, a kind of okayness in which one feels at-ease regardless of outer circumstances. It implies an absence of regret. No energy wasted wishing things were different from what they are. No dwelling on stuff we can't control.

In everyday terms, santosha counsels us to create conditions in our lives that are conducive to maintaining contentment: a peaceful environment, harmonious relationships, and material comfort. It also suggests that we cultivate within ourselves the kind of temperament, disposition, perspective, and attitude that naturally breeds contentment.

In a state of deep and authentic contentment there is no craving for things we don't have, no obsession with objects of desire, no nagging feeling that something is missing. Santosha is also likely to give rise to desirable qualities such as gratitude and appreciation. It might even nudge us to cherish the little things we do have and typically take for granted.

It's not hard to imagine the difference between speaking and acting from a contented disposition instead of one characterized by disgruntled agitation, restlessness, and resentment.

We've all been to both places; we only need to remember how we responded to people and events under each condition. The karmic consequences are obvious.

It should also be noted that contentment is not synonymous with complacency or indifference. Being content does not mean we don't bother correcting wrongs, reversing injustices, curtailing cruelty, or preventing harm to others. On the contrary, it's a fine platform for unselfish action.

Tapas

No, not the small plates of food in Spanish restaurants, but the Sanskrit term that derives from a root meaning burn or heat. As a niyama, tapas points to austerity, self-discipline, and the control of energy. Anyone who's delved into the more esoteric corners of yoga in India knows that extreme forms of tapas are employed by certain ascetics—standing on one leg interminably, going without food or water for long periods of time, exposing one's unprotected body to heat and cold, shoving long needles through skin, etc.—for the ostensibly spiritual purpose of training the body to generate internal energy like a battery.

As an everyday matter for non-hermits, such mortification is not only impractical and unappealing but potentially harmful. No need for torturous self-denial. "The body is not to be brutally beaten and broken," state Prabhavananda and Isherwood. "It is to be handled firmly but considerately, as one handles a horse." The body is, after all, a "vehicle for awakening," as Buddha reportedly said.

For the vast majority of humanity, tapas is best understood as discipline, self-control, and common-sense restraint. Some commentators apply it to the occasional withdrawal of the senses, as in practices such as meditation, fasting, silent retreats, and sabbaths. There's a reason every spiritual tradition has such rituals. The purpose is to preserve and regenerate energy instead of expending it wastefully, making more of it available for nobler purposes than the enjoyment of sensory pleasures. It's like a spiritual version of the law of thermodynamics: conserve energy and redirect it toward the holy.

Tapas can also apply directly to karmically beneficial action; it takes discipline and self-training to behave consistently in accord with moral virtues. Think of it as comparable to the passionate dedication of artists and athletes who sacrifice ordinary pleasures to run sprints or play scales over and over again, often pushing the body and mind to extremes for the sake of athletic or artistic excellence. For readers of this book, the payoff for discipline, restraint, and willpower are spiritual attainment and good karma.

One more level of tapas: exercising disciplined self-restraint when self-centered, decadent, mean-spirited, or other karmically harmful impulses arise.

Svadhyaya

Literally, "self-study," svadhyaya has been interpreted in several ways. The most common is the deep study of sacred texts. For Georg Feuerstein, a scholar of the Indic traditions, svadhyaya "denotes one's own delving into the hidden meanings of the scriptures."

The potentially transformative effects of contemplative study have been extolled by all spiritual traditions, and methods such as Christianity's *lectio divina* ("divine reading") have been developed to maximize the benefits of persistent, ever-deepening excavation of wisdom.

It should be emphasized that the value of such study is not merely intellectual. The intent is to persistently turn our attention to the higher reaches of spiritual attainment, and to show us how to shift from understanding to action. The point is to discern the deepest and most practical teachings and apply them to our lives—to internalize the insights of the ages, so they'll act on our minds and hearts like healing elixirs. Beyond that, the ultimate aim is to put the texts aside and discover what the words describe—in modern parlance, to walk the talk. As the classic Buddhist metaphor teaches us, there's a difference between seeing the finger that points to the moon and seeing the moon itself. The best of the sacred texts point beyond themselves to realities whose true value comes only from direct experience.

Svadhyaya extends to other forms of self-study as well, such as diligent enquiry into our own psychological dynamics. It urges introspection. It encourages us to discern the thought patterns, emotional tendencies, personality traits, and hidden motivations that underly our actions, and then to discover how we can improve.

Ultimately, the purpose of svadhyaya is self-knowledge, and that includes both acute awareness of our unique little selves—the self that's different from other little selves—and also the realization of the big Self, the unbound identity we share with all of existence and is called by different names by different mystical traditions. More on that in a later chapter.

Ishvara pranidhana

This, the last of the five niyamas, is a call to include the element of bhakti, or devotion, in one's spiritual repertoire. The term Ishvara is used to connote Supreme Being or Ultimate Reality—the divine either as manifest in one of its infinite number of forms or as formless, boundless, and transcendent. In most cases it signifies the former, that is, a specific personification of divinity. Pranidhana means to devote to, dedicate to, surrender to, or affix to. Hence, devotion to God, dedication to the Lord, surrender to the Almighty, always with the provision that individuals are free to choose their own ishtadevata, i.e., their preferred form of the divine. In our globalized modern world, that choice would encompass not only the enormous number of Hindu deities but any focus of Buddhist, Christian, Muslim, Jewish, or other devotion that suits the individual.

In non-sectarian terms, which suit many people more than religious ones, Ishvara pranidhana can be interpreted as devotion to one's spiritual development, or being attuned to, and humbly yielding to, a Higher Power. Think, for example, of two of the famous Twelve Steps (if you prefer, by all means, edit the masculine pronouns): "Made a decision to turn our will and our lives over to the care of God as we understood Him," and, "Sought through prayer and meditation to improve our conscious contact with God as we understood Him, praying only for knowledge of His will for us and the power to carry that out."

Ishvara pranidhana encourages us to cultivate the Big View and see ourselves and our ever-changing circumstances as best we can in the context of an unimaginably complex evolutionary drama, which we can control only to an extremely limited degree. It is both elevating and humbling to realize that, on the one hand, we are divine beings and, on the other, minute specks in a landscape of infinite time, endless space, and unlimited power. Yielding to that perspective, even to a small degree, smooths the edges of egotism and invites us to offer up our actions in service of the greater good rather than always grasping for things we crave.

What Would Buddha Do?

The importance of behaving in accord with the highest principles of morality and ethics permeated the teachings of Siddhartha Gautama, the great teacher known to history as Buddha. It also permeates the voluminous literature that developed over the centuries since Buddha delivered his first dharma talk (to an audience of five, tradition has it) about twenty-six centuries ago. Virtuous behavior weaves in and out the Buddhist canon as both contributing to the attainment of nirvana, the highest state of awareness, and as a product of that development.

This is clearly seen in The Eightfold Path, which from the start capped off Buddha's Four Noble Truths, showing the way out of the discontent or suffering that marks the ordinary human condition. The eight components include right speech, right livelihood, and right action. Those virtues have been the subject of analysis, interpretation, and debate ever since Buddha himself left the scene. They're more complicated than they appear to be, and certainly more so than they were in the simple societies of Buddha's day. That said, most takes on right speech come down to speaking truthfully, kindly, and compassionately without causing harm with one's words, and right livelihood means earning one's living in ways that contribute to the overall good and not through labor that causes suffering, violence, or moral degradation.

As for right action, well, in a sense that's what ethical systems and behavioral codes are all about. One possible answer within the Buddhist framework is the Six Paramitas. Known variously in English as the Sublime Virtues, the Transcendent Perfections, and other lofty terms, the paramitas are similar to the niyamas in that they are not commands or decrees, but positive qualities, or virtues, that aspirants are urged to cultivate. Also like the yamas and niyamas, the six paramitas are mutually enhancing; they interact like organs in a body, such that, as Thich Nhat Hanh puts it, "if you practice one paramita deeply, you practice all six." And, like most behavioral precepts, their real-life applications are not always obvious; hence, the need to interpret them and flesh them out.

Dana paramita

Dana is almost universally translated as generosity. It points to a spirit of compassionate giving, ideally without hesitation, calculation, egotism, or the expectation of getting something in return. When we think of someone as being generous it's usually because they give more expensive gifts than they can really afford, or they dispense handsome bequests to loved ones and donations to charities, or they entertain lavishly. Needless to say, there are other expressions of generosity that might be more karmically potent. Giving one's time to worthy causes or a neighbor in need, for example, or rolling up one's sleeves to help a stranded driver change a tire, or cancelling a lunch date to take an injured stranger to an emergency room, or giving someone a bed for the night.

Deeper still, what about the generosity of listening attentively to someone who needs to be heard? Holding the hand of a suffering person? Reaching out with sympathetic kindness to someone mourning a loss? Offering sound advice and useful information to someone struggling to make a decision? Sharing your expertise with a novice?

Even better is to do any of the above without an agenda—not even hoping for a round of applause or a thank you note. That's the kind of charity all religions value the most. Why would the laws of karma be any different? As we'll see, intention and motivation matter as much, if not more, than behavior.

Life presents us with frequent moments when we get to choose how generous we'll be: in restaurants, in taxis, when solicited by charities and worthy causes, at gift-giving time, when asked for assistance, etc. We can stretch our usual limits, or we can withhold. We all know how much better we feel when we do the former, assuming we can open our hands and hearts in a safe, non-risky manner. Religious literature is filled with teaching stories that contrast poor people who offer strangers a meager meal from their humble supplies with wealthy people who are stingy and unwelcoming. It goes without saying which of the two is best rewarded.

If you prefer an example from a master storyteller, you can't do better than to revisit Charles Dickens's *A Christmas Carol*, either the novel itself or one of the many movie versions. Author and meditation teacher Dean Sluyter helped me see that in an insightful series of articles for *Tricycle* magazine[42] in which he linked each of the paramitas to great works of literature. The Ebenezer Scrooge we meet at the beginning of the tale is the embodiment of generosity's opposite, a heartless miser whom Dickens describes as "squeezing, wrenching, grasping, scraping, clutching, covetous." That Scrooge is one of the least happy creeps in all of literature. Then come the famous Christmas Eve visits from Scrooge's former partner and fellow grinch, Jacob Marley, and from the Ghosts of Christmas Past, Present, and Yet to Come. By Christmas morning, Scrooge is transformed into the very picture of dana, "as good a friend, as good a master, and as good a man, as the good old city knew, or any other good old city, town, or borough, in the good old world." After bestowing gifts to those he'd denied and exploited in the past, he walks about town and finds that "everything could yield him pleasure."

It's doubtful that Dickens had ever heard the word karma, but he understood the principle and knew that we get what we give and that we can all learn to give more.

Sila paramita

This one refers to morality in general and encompasses the entire scope of ethical conduct and virtuous behavior. To put it succinctly, as Paramahansa Yogananda's guru, Sri Yukteswar, often did: Learn to behave!

It goes without saying that there are numerous versions of exactly which behaviors sila pertains to, and which moral code ought to be the standard. The usual suspects—kindness, compassion, etc.—are typically invoked by commentators. Broadly speaking, it's safe to say that a karmically sound standard would be to perform actions that reduce suffering and increase happiness, harmony, and spiritual awakening.

Thich Nhat Hanh equates sila with the observance of what he calls The Five Mindfulness Trainings, namely:

1. "Protecting the lives of human beings, animals, vegetables, and minerals."
2. "Prevent the exploitation by humans of other living beings and of nature."
3. "Protect children and adults from sexual abuse."
4. "Practice deep listening and loving speech."
5. "Mindful consumption," referring to wholesome food, drink, and other forms of consumption.

By living these trainings, says Thay (as his followers call him), "we protect ourselves and the people we love."[43]

Kshanti paramita

Typically defined as patience or forbearance, kshanti is sometimes held up as an ideal response to life's challenges. Our patience is tried on a regular basis, by needy family members, boring acquaintances, trouble-prone friends, annoying coworkers, demanding bosses, tiresome political arguments, traffic jams, automated customer service, and on and on. We know what happens when we succumb to impatience. We say things we regret. We hurt people's feelings. We don't get the desired outcome. Kshanti instead urges us to remain calm, collected, and centered.

Beyond ordinary patience, kshanti implies the ability to endure pain, adversity, and difficulties without overreacting or responding impulsively. Notably, Thich Nhat Hanh prefers the term "inclusiveness" to other translations. By inclusive he means something different from the word's current use as a social ideal in conditions of diversity. He means responding to circumstances with a big-hearted "capacity to receive, embrace, and transform."

He invokes Buddha's guidelines for developing that quality: "maitri (love), karuna (compassion), mudita (joy), and upeksha (equanimity)."[44]

We can all reach back to our own experience and remember challenging times when we kept our wits about us and other times when we lost it. Which did you regret? Keeping our cool is not only better for our mental and physical health; it also improves our chances of making wise, sensitive, pragmatic decisions in the heat of the moment. If you can't find proof in your own life, think of athletes, executives, or first responders who have to react with maximum skill under enormous pressure. Who do you want in charge when the chips are down? Who do you give the ball to if you're the coach? Contrast those cool cucumbers with nervous wrecks and impetuous, reckless swashbucklers. If you need Shakespearean help, Dean Sluyter suggests Macbeth, who was destined to be king but couldn't patiently await his turn. Instead, he charged into bloody murder and hopped onto the throne with unseemly haste. To drive home the miserable consequences of Macbeth's non-kshanti behavior, the Bard allows the king and the conniving Lady Macbeth no transformation, no redemption, no happy karmic relief.

Virya paramita

Virya means diligence and, like all meaningful virtues, its range of application is broad. On an everyday level, it can mean doing what has to be done, without resentment, without annoyance, and without compromising effort or care. You might be familiar with the classic Zen saying, "Before enlightenment, chop wood and carry water. After enlightenment, chop wood and carry water." There are layers of meaning in that adage, and one of them is: whatever your state of consciousness, however lofty your perspective, fulfill your ordinary responsibilities impeccably. Another

Buddhist teaching is to do everything as if the Buddha himself were standing next to you, watching.

Virya is also taken to mean the application of assiduous effort and conscientious persistence on the spiritual path. We're called upon to persevere, to apply ourselves consistently and not slack off or become distracted. To keep our eyes on the prize of realization. It also means being meticulous about our behavior, i.e., to speak and act in accord with the highest ethical standards, and to diligently cultivate wholesome traits while rejecting their opposites.

Dhyana paramita

Dhyana, which also happens to be the seventh of the eight limbs of classical yoga, is Sanskrit for meditation (when yoga was exported to other parts of Asia, dhyana became chan in Chinese and zen in Japanese). That it's considered one of the supreme virtues indicates the centrality of meditation in the Buddhist constellation. At this point, the benefits of meditative practice are widely known in the West. Indeed, readers of a book like this might already meditate regularly, and if they don't, they certainly know it would be a good idea to do so.

We'll have more to say about this in chapter 7. Here, let's take the lead of various commentators and expand the perspective on dhyana from sitting practice alone to a kind of meditative approach to action as well. Perhaps the paramita is intended to suggest the cultivation in daily life of qualities we associate with meditation: ease, non-judgmental receptivity, steady focus, full attention to whatever is present, neutrality toward extraneous sensations, acceptance of all that arises without clinging, grasping, or attachment. This approach evokes the Taoist concept of *wu-wei*—effortless action in alignment with the natural flow of things.

Prajna paramita

Discernment seems to be the most common translation of prajna, with wisdom close behind. In its highest form, prajna (like pragya in the Hindu tradition) refers to the realization of one's essential nature and its inextricable unity with all that is. On that level, it can be understood as discerning what is true, real, and permanent, as distinct from the ordinary perception of transient phenomena.

But why not apply the principle of wise discernment to our understanding of the people and situations in our lives? The more we perceive things as they really are, the greater insight we have into the karmic circumstances confronting us, and the more acutely we perceive the connections among the various elements, the more fruitful our decisions will be, and the wiser our choices. Prajna suggests rising above the ignorance and delusion that invariably lead to karmic mistakes.

Some commentators divide prajna into three components or stages, essentially: 1) taking in information alertly, attentively, and astutely, 2) reflecting on what you've taken in, contemplatively, fastidiously, and discerningly, 3) absorbing and internalizing the knowledge to make it part of you.

Protect and Serve

Perhaps the most potent action one can undertake to move the karmic scorecard in a favorable direction is to serve others. Every spiritual tradition calls upon its followers to devote time, energy, and resources to helping those in need. In the West we call it charity. In India, it goes by the Sanskrit term seva, which is usually defined as selfless service. That modifier, selfless, is crucial; the karmic impact of a charitable act is either diminished or enhanced by the amount of ego that drives it.

Swami Prabhavananda describes the promise of seva this

way: "Through the practice of nonattachment and selfless service the devotee frees himself from the wheel of cause and effect, deed and reward, and obtains the Infinite." Actions that benefit others can be as pro forma as dropping a dollar in a donation basket. They can be merely transactional, as when a person of means assuages his guilt—or, if she's religious, wants to get right with God—by writing a tax-deductible check. But, as we'll explore in greater depth later in the book, our attitude matters a great deal. It's not just what we do, it's why we do it. Selfish motivation, whether from a public figure who wants to burnish his reputation or a philanthropist seeking immortality by having her name on a building or a big tipper showing off to a date, can vulgarize an outwardly generous action and thereby reduce the value of a karmic advantage. It's like getting flagged for an unsportsmanlike conduct penalty after a long gain in a football game. On the other end of the spectrum, a sincere, heartfelt, noble attitude can make an ordinary thoughtful action—helping an overloaded shopper carry a package, giving a homeless person the rest of your sandwich, shoveling your aging neighbor's driveway—into something like a holy offering.

Getting the ego out of the way is the essence of the time-honored path of karma yoga. It means not expecting or anticipating rewards—not plaudits, not recognition, not even a wave from the driver you let into the lane ahead of you. It means, in the language of the Bhagavad Gita, not being attached to the fruits of our actions. Non-attachment, it's important to add, does not mean you don't care whether your actions produce a desired result. It means doing what you do attentively, skillfully, passionately, with no thought of the future and no personal stake in the outcome. And that, paradoxically, is how you get the most out of it, both in practical terms and karmic benefit.

"If a man works without any selfish motive, does he not gain something?" Swami Vivekananda asked rhetorically with respect to karma yoga, and his answer is, "Yes, he gains the highest benefit." Why? Because giving produces returns on investment; actions that arise from genuine love, kindness, and generosity bring their own rewards. New parents quickly discover this truth, hence Vivekananda advises, "In whatever you do for a particular person, city, or state, assume the same attitude towards it as you do towards your children—expect nothing in return." Then he raises the stakes by posing an even bigger challenge: "[R]emember that it is a privilege to help others," therefore "be grateful that the poor man is there, so that by making a gift to him you are able to help yourself. . . . Be thankful that you are allowed to exercise your power of benevolence and mercy in the world."

Because, for most humans, "What's in it for me?" comes to mind more readily than "What's the right thing to do?" the ideal of selfless action might seem like too much to expect of ourselves. Too idealistic. Too sacrificial. Too "religious." Too big a leap of faith. But think back to times in your own life when you were enlisted to serve someone in need, perhaps with little notice in an emergency situation. How did it feel? Was there not an element of fulfillment in it? A sense of well-being? Peace? Even joy? There are a zillion testimonies to that effect.

Here's mine. Late in my father's life, when I was alone with him in his home one evening, he suddenly started shuddering with chills. I threw a blanket over him. I gave him hot tea. I massaged his neck. Then he lost control of his bowels and started to teeter. I called 911, and as I waited for an ambulance to arrive, I wiped his legs clean of feces and helped him remove his soiled underpants and put on pajama bottoms. I returned from the hospital close to dawn. I scrubbed the floor, took out the trash, ate something, and fell into bed. Suddenly, in my exhaustion, a surge of grace came over me. I felt a profound contentment, followed by something odd: gratitude. I couldn't figure out why. Then I realized that I'd been thrust into the purest act of giving I'd ever experienced, and I hadn't had a single thought about myself in about six hours.

I once heard a guru say, "If you want to be depressed, think about yourself all the time." The corollary is what I experienced with my father. In the words of Nobel Laureate Rabindranath Tagore, "I slept and dreamt that life was joy / I woke and saw that life was service / I acted and behold! service was joy."

Need proof? As it happens, there is considerable scientific evidence that giving produces almost instant karma in the form of feelgood neurochemicals like serotonin and dopamine. What's come to be seen as a sanctimonious cliché, "It is more blessed to give than to receive," might be demonstrably true. Studies show that people who devote time to helping others tend to be, on average, happier, more satisfied, and more optimistic. They also live measurably longer and healthier (less stress, lower blood pressure, etc.). That's probably why Mother Teresa reportedly had terminally ill patients pray for one another instead of for themselves.

Stephen Post, a leading researcher in positive psychology and author of *Why Good Things Happen to Good People*, has studied the impact of volunteerism on the volunteers themselves. One of his findings suggests that the positive effects of serving others when one is young (in this case high school age) last at least into midlife. It doesn't take much; a few hours a week produces measurable benefit. And you don't have to stray far afield; surely, wherever you are, your kindness and generosity are needed by someone close by.

Before we leave this subject, let's address a common source of hesitation. To be karmically beneficial, service doesn't have to be grim or arduous. Doing good doesn't have to be sacrificial. Acting selflessly is not the same as self-denial. On the contrary, service is most effective when the servers enjoy what they're doing and can draw on their talents and skills. When you think about it, why would doing something helpful in accord with your interests and gifts produce any less good karma than doing something tedious or grueling? You'll certainly do it a lot better. "Don't ask yourself what the world needs," advised Howard Thurman, the revered theologian, pastor, and civil rights leader. "Ask yourself what makes you come alive, and then go do that, because what the world needs is people who have come alive."

Service begins by placing the thought "How can I help?" ahead of "What's in it for me?" Do that and opportunities will naturally arise, and exactly what's in it for you will become obvious once you take up the necessary action. Just leave your ego at home.

Cultivating the Good

Let's face it, doing the right thing isn't always easy. Not only is it sometimes hard to know what the right thing is, but behavioral formulas that seem direct and unequivocal can be confusing in practice, and even when we know for certain what the right thing is, we're not always willing or able to do it. Chapter one, verse 33 of the Yoga Sutras, for example, says that one way to achieve peace of mind, or a quiet mental state, is to cultivate friendliness to the happy, compassion for the unhappy, delight for the virtuous, and indifference toward the wicked. Simple enough.

That is, until you run into a very happy person and feelings of envy rise up in you. Or you meet a miserable, downcast acquaintance and find yourself sinking into *schadenfreude* (German for taking pleasure in another's misfortune), even as you outwardly express sympathy. Or someone is praised for being virtuous and you resent them for getting all the attention. As for indifference in the face of evil, is that really a virtue? Commentators seem to be in agreement that "indifference" in this context does not mean apathy or coldhearted non-concern. It means, rather, maintaining calm, or equanimity, even if the situation calls for taking action to prevent harm. The point is, simple guidelines are not always easy to follow.

Sometimes the mind knows the right thing to do, but the

body doesn't want to cooperate. Sometimes, our emotions overrule our will. Instinct can overpower intellect. We can trick ourselves into believing that a selfish action—one that satisfies a craving or gives voice to anger, retribution, or jealousy—is the right action, the truly good action, the only proper action in that situation. We're human, and therefore imperfect, and therefore prone to mistakes and self-delusion. And we reap the karma accordingly.

Remember, the niyamas and the paramitas are practices, not laws to be obeyed. The latter might sometimes be called perfections, but that doesn't mean you have to be perfect to practice them, and it certainly doesn't mean that you have to wait until you've achieved perfection in them (if that's even possible) before benefiting from cultivating them. Paramita practice, after all, is part of the training for women and men who have taken the bodhisattva vow to delay their own liberation in order to help others along the path. If those vow-taking souls are works in progress, the rest of us certainly are. So, when you fall short you might want to apply those very paramitas to yourself. We all deserve a little patience and forbearance. We all need to extend to ourselves the compassion, kindness, and generosity of spirit we aspire to offer others.

The task of creating favorable karma as we move forward in life requires replacing old habits with new ones, and that takes time. Research suggests that cementing a new habit takes a lot of repetition, in some cases for a matter of days and in others for weeks or months. And consistency matters. Each time we do something, we not only sow the seeds of future karma, but we also train the mind. We carve new neural pathways—grooves of thought so to speak—and as a result, performing the action next time is a tad easier. Repetition also makes it much more likely that, in time, the behavior will occur spontaneously. Experience suggests that, if our hearts are in the right place, doing the right thing becomes easier and easier. Which doesn't mean we'll never revert to old, less desirable habits; some of those grooves run quite deep. Patience is obligatory even as we hold ourselves to high standards.

Meanwhile, here are some ideas for speeding up progress toward your behavioral aspirations:

- Make a list of the virtues you would like most to develop, or that you think you need most to cultivate. The goal would be to make them your default behaviors.
- Each week, choose one of those aspirations to focus on for the ensuing seven days and challenge yourself to choose it over less worthy, but possibly juicier, alternatives whenever you're faced with the choice.
- Monitor yourself, perhaps by reviewing the events of the day when going to bed each night. Identify the circumstances and personal traits that made it difficult to express that virtue. Write down ways you can do better moving forward.
- Employ the power of imagination to train your subconscious mind to initiate the desirable behavior when appropriate. Many athletes and other high performers use guided visualization to "rehearse" inwardly. They essentially program their minds by imagining themselves coming through with excellence in typical circumstances. Doing this frequently and regularly embeds the ideal action in the mind for transfer into speech and action.

Simply choose a trait you want to cultivate, set aside a comfortable period of time (perhaps 5-10 minutes), close your eyes, use your preferred method of calming the mind and body (meditation, mindfulness, breathwork, prayer, etc.) and imagine yourself exhibiting the desired behavior in typical situations. Observe yourself saying and doing the right things and notice how it feels.

Repeat as needed. Note: Experts advise visualizing plausible behavior, not some out-of-reach fantasy that would cause your subconscious mind to say, "Yeah, right! Dream on, pal."

One aide to those practices is to recall a time in your life when you exhibited the desired trait, whether spontaneously or through effort. Sit with the memory for a bit, then visualize yourself demonstrating the same quality in the present. Understand that the traits we consider karmically desirable are all innate; they come to us naturally under the right conditions if we allow them to. We're all more competent at some virtues than others, and some of us are extraordinarily gifted in one or the other, just as everyone can run and jump and sing and dance (barring illness or incapacity), but there are only a few Olympians and rock stars. We own every virtue; we just need to wake up the desired qualities and summon them to action like sleeping soldiers.

If you have difficulty remembering times when you manifested a particular trait, think of a role model—someone who exemplifies the quality and whose behavior you can emulate. It could be a friend or a family member, a mentor, an admired public figure, a celebrated person from history, even a fictional character from a novel or a movie. If you need a cinematic model of a convert to selfless service, consider Rick, the Humphrey Bogart character in *Casablanca*. Through the course of the film, we see a hardened cynic become transformed into a responsible citizen who's noble enough to sacrifice being with the one great love of his life (Ingrid Berman) to serve a higher purpose. "It doesn't take much to see that the problems of three little people don't amount to a hill of beans in this crazy world," he says, famously, and off he goes to do his bit to defeat the Nazi menace. If the likes of Rick can overcome his resistance to the dormant righteousness within him, so can the rest of us.

Dharma Bonds

The concept of dharma, for which there is no adequate English equivalent, is intimately linked to karma. The term is often translated as duty, but duty doesn't quite measure up. It carries the taint of earnest obligation, which tends to rub moderns the wrong way and can be used to abuse and exploit. As Swami Tyagananda of the Boston Vedanta Society says, "Few other words in the literatures of the world are filled with such depth in meaning and fewer still have been the cause of so much misunderstanding and conflict."

Dharma derives from a Sanskrit root meaning to uphold or sustain. Something is dharmic if it upholds what is natural, life-enhancing, and harmonious, thereby sustaining individual well-being and the collective good. Dharma has been compared to a ship's rudder, because it keeps society balanced and moving in the desired direction.

Acting in accord with our personal dharma is considered so important that the Bhagavad Gita says, somewhat startlingly, "Better is death in following one's own dharma; the dharma of another brings danger." You read that correctly. It was considered better to die and come back in a fresh new body than to degrade your karma and disrupt social harmony by crossing into the wrong lane. In the context of that era, following one's dharma meant honoring the norms and customs of the existing social structure, which included the varna system, a division of labor in which specific responsibilities were assigned to each of four occupational categories. (As noted in chapter two, the varna system later devolved into the hereditary caste system that has been such a stain on Indian society.)

For our use, the injunction about honoring one's dharma can be interpreted as a call to authenticity, along the lines of this saying attributed to the Buddha: "Know well what leads you forward and what holds you back, and choose the path that leads to wisdom." In other words, understand your personal nature, study your propensities and tendencies, and identify the most virtuous, life-enhancing, socially harmonious, and responsible mode of behavior for each of the various roles you play: parent, spouse, offspring, sibling, professional, employee or employer, and so forth. The formula is simple: adhering to dharma produces favorable karma.

Given the complexities of modern life, determining one's dharma in any given circumstance can be tricky stuff. I've seen people tie themselves in knots trying to identify their dharmically ideal career path, i.e., their true calling, or trying to figure out whether so-and-so would be a dharmic marriage partner. Some of them wished, not entirely facetiously, that they lived in a society where such things are determined by custom or by elders. We have too many choices, they felt, and it would be so much easier if our lives were fastidiously circumscribed. It's also sometimes hard to distinguish what seems to be our dharma from an ego trip, a delusion, or a convenient fiction.

One approach is to look back on our lives and identify patterns. Where have things gone wrong? Which decisions have led repeatedly to "bad luck"? What didn't turn out as intended? When did you meet with the stiffest resistance? What damaged your relationships? The answers might point to ways you have not acted in accord with your dharma.

On the flip side: When have things gone splendidly right? When did you have "good luck"? When did things flow smoothly? Which of your actions drew the most support and respect from others? Which ones have led to the greatest rewards? Those were probably times when you were in sync with dharma, and when your actions honored both your own integrity and the dignity of others in your orbit.

Here is a traditional teaching story, origin unknown (I've

seen it used by Hindus, Buddhists, and others) that captures the meaning of dharma and depicts an ideal to emulate even if it's unreachable.

Two monks on a journey step into a shallow pool of water to wash up. The elder monk sees a scorpion struggling in the water. Knowing that scorpions can't swim, he scoops it up to place it on shore out of harm's way. But the arachnid stings him. He loses his grip, and the scorpion falls back into the water. The monk tries again, and again he's stung, and again the scorpion splashes into the dangerous pool.

The pattern repeats a few more times until, finally, the monk manages to toss the scorpion onto the shore. As the animal scampers away, the younger monk begins nursing the elder's wounds and pondering what he's just witnessed. Finally, he gets up the nerve to ask: "Honorable one, why did you let that scorpion sting you over and over again?"

The wise monk replies: "The scorpion's dharma is to sting. It is my dharma to serve all sentient beings."

Enemies Near and Far

Replacing bad habits with karmically benevolent behavior is seldom like flipping a toggle switch. It's more like Mark Twain's famous statement, "Giving up smoking is the easiest thing in the world. I know because I've done it thousands of times." Consistency takes time. It requires ongoing attention, self-assessment, and self-monitoring.

One form of self-betrayal is particularly interesting in this context: the Buddhist concept of the "near enemy." The term refers to a personal quality or mental state that resembles a virtuous trait but is actually a distortion of it. A near enemy *appears* to be similar to the desired attribute, or even identical with it, but is actually quite different in effect. It can, therefore, undermine our ability to act in the most karmically desirable way. This makes the near enemy much more insidious than the "far enemy," which is a quality that occupies the opposite end of the spectrum from a virtue to which we aspire. Because they're the antithesis of desirable behavior, far enemies are easy to discern. They are like the governments of the United States and China; everyone knows they're in direct opposition to one another. Near enemies are more like spies and counterspies, stealthy adversaries who masquerade as allies.

According to scholars I reached out to, the concept of near enemy isn't found in the canonical Buddhist texts. It came along later as part of the tradition of commentary and elaboration. Its most prevalent use has been in relation to the interpretation of the *Brahmaviharas*, also known as the Four Immeasurables. These are essential virtues the tradition urges us to cultivate: loving-kindness (metta), compassion (karuna), sympathetic joy (mudita), and equanimity (upekkha). They each have far enemies and near enemies:

~The far enemy of loving-kindness is hatred or ill will.

~The far enemy of compassion is cruelty or callousness.

~The far enemy of sympathetic joy (which means, essentially, rejoicing in another's happiness and good fortune) is envy, jealousy, or resentment.

~The far enemy of equanimity is agitation, anxiety, or inner disturbance.

Those enemies are easy to identify, are they not? It would take a lot of self-deception for someone to confuse them with the karmically beneficial behavior they're trying to nurture. Near enemies are far more devious. The near enemies of loving-kindness are qualities such as attachment, control, possessiveness, clinging, and dependency. It's easy to mistake those near enemies for the kind of selfless, unconditional love to which the term *metta* points.

The near enemies of compassion might include pity, condescension, and smugness, or perhaps offering up a superficial expression of concern but failing to act accordingly. Again, it's easy to confuse such near enemies with the brahmavihara of karuna, which implies a heartfelt intent to alleviate the suffering of another being.

The near enemies of sympathetic (aka appreciative or empathetic) joy might be a forced, insincere expression of delight that masks the envy, jealousy, or disinterest lurking in the shadows of the heart. Haven't we all pretended to be thrilled by someone's good fortune because we knew it was expected of us and we wanted to show off how bighearted we are? Similarly, we might express exuberant happiness at the achievement of an individual or a group, when what we're really feeling is pride because the victorious person is a family member or the group represents our company or town. In such instances, the near enemy allows us to pat ourselves on the back, but it's not the empathetic delight that mudita calls us to.

Finally, the near enemies of equanimity would include indifference and apathy. It's very easy to mistake an utter lack of interest for the imperturbable state of upekkha, in which inner peace is a platform for actions that serve the greater good.

A phenomenon well-known to psychotherapists is a close cousin to the near enemy. It's when we take one of our own most admirable traits too far or unknowingly misdirect it. By so doing, we essentially turn a strength into a weakness and perhaps convert a karmically beneficial attribute into an action that creates not-so-beneficial karma.

One of the most compassionate people I've ever known—a veritable saint if you ask her friends—has periodically turned her life into a spectacular mess by being *so* compassionate, *so* non-judgmental, *so* understanding, that she fails to hold people accountable for egregious behavior. "She's incredibly empathic," a mutual friend said of her. "She has an amazing ability to comprehend *why* people do the things they do, and it's a beautiful thing to see. But sometimes it comes across as just making excuses." As result, she and others have been taken advantage of, triggering anger and resentment from her friends and family members.

Someone else I knew was the poster child for generosity. A deeply spiritual and loving soul, he worked diligently on non-attachment, constantly trying to remove his ego and personal desires from his actions. In his spiritual community he was admired and beloved. But he was also known as an easy mark. If someone was in need, he'd write a check, no questions asked. He gave people loans and didn't always get paid back. In his mind, pursuing repayment would have been an unseemly materialistic thing to do. This all might have made sense if he were wealthy. But he wasn't, and his wife and children, forced to do without things they wanted, did not consider his generosity a saintly virtue. Their family tension was not exactly good karma.

Knowing that imposters like near enemies are lurking in the shadows of virtue should keep us vigilant. It's a reminder to keep an eye on ourselves, to exercise discernment, and to strive for authenticity if the aim is to do the karmically right thing consistently. Knowing how easy it is to deceive ourselves also serves to keep us humble. We may want to be angels, but none of us can dance on the head of a pin, and, as G.K. Chesterton memorably said, "Angels can fly because they take themselves so lightly."

This suggests that developing a good sense of humor might be as helpful as cultivating right behavior. The ability to guffaw at our foibles and howl at our hapless humanness goes a long way to make the path of karmic rehab an enjoyable adventure rather than a bleak, guilt-ridden slog. A good laugh, especially at our own expense, can be as spiritually healing as prayer—maybe more so if the prayer is insincere. A comedian[45] once said that sincerity is everything in life—and if you can fake that, you've got it made. It would seem that doing the best we can with a purity of intention and a lightness of foot will create better karma than grimly going through the motions of virtuous behavior. In the cosmic restaurant of karma, we can order off the menu a la carte, but we'll still be served only what we deserve.

5
Don't Do the Wrong Thing

"He who shits on the road will meet flies on his return." –*Mr. Natural (Robert Crumb)*

In a famous TV sketch, the late comedian Bob Newhart plays a therapist who responds to every problem his patient presents with a two-word solution: "Stop it!"

That's good advice when we're about to do something that's bound to produce bad karma. Creating a favorable karmic future is not just about acting virtuously; it also means rejecting behavior that will whack us on the rebound like a boxer's speed bag. Put another way, sometimes the best route to doing the right thing is not to do the wrong thing.

Over the centuries, strict moralists and religious leaders have been all too eager to tell us what not to do. Don'ts, mustn'ts, and thou shalt nots are among the first things we hear as children, and much as we don't like hearing them, we often end up repeating them to ourselves internally and then out loud to our own kids. We need don'ts. They're a curb on our worst instincts. They spare us a lot of misery, and they're necessary for family harmony and social cohesion. The rule of law, after all, is based on what we want citizens not to do. Like most things, don'ts can be taken too far; authoritarians turn reasonable don'ts into repressive, unnatural prohibitions with draconian punishment for offenders—only to be secretly subverted and, in due time, openly rebelled against.

Those are not the kind of don'ts we'll consider here. As we did with the *dos* in the previous chapter, we'll eschew commands and decrees and turn instead to guidelines from the traditions in which karma is foundational.

The Yamas

As noted earlier, the first two limbs of the eight-limbed path of classical Yoga consist of behavioral precepts. We took them in reverse order, covering the second limb, the five niyamas, in the previous chapter. Now we'll look at the first of Patanjali's limbs, the five *yamas*. Usually translated as restraints or abstentions, the yamas are essentially forms of behavior it's a good idea to avoid, or at least restrict. If you've read the Upanishads, you might be wondering if there's a connection between the yamas, lower case, and Yama, upper case, aka the Lord of Death in Hindu mythology. One link can be found in classical depictions of Yama, where he holds a lasso in one hand. He uses it to extract the soul from a deceased body to send it on its way. Hence, some interpret lower case yama as a means of freeing one's higher nature from the limitations of bodily urges and base desires.

That Patanjali chose to lead with behaviors to resist, when he might have flipped them over to their positive side as recommended actions, suggests that the ancient sages were well aware of the power of human urges to lead us astray. In his massive text, *The Yoga Tradition*, Georg Feuerstein puts it this way: "These moral attitudes are meant to bring our instinctual life under control." It comes down to reining in the wild horses of the senses (to use a classic yogic metaphor) so they might be directed toward higher purposes and more enduring fulfillment rather than the fleeting delights that so often lead to attachments, undesirable habits, and karmic troubles.

For the full-time renunciate yogis whom, it is believed, Patanjali was addressing, complete and unequivocal self-control would have been advocated. But the yamas are meant to be applicable to everyone at all times, as the verse (2, 31) that follows their naming indicates: "These great vows are universal, not limited by class, place, time or circumstance."[46] For non-renunciates living in the world of families and worldly obligations, modification and discernment are needed. Feuerstein refers to yama as "moral discipline." This suggests that adhering to the yamas requires ongoing attention and effort, making them something of a moving target, perhaps never to be permanently bulls-eyed. Let's look at them in the order in which Patanjali placed them.

Ahimsa

The first of the yamas numerically, *ahimsa*, might also be considered first in the sense of being primary, fundamental, or most important—the first of the first. Most often translated as nonviolence, ahimsa goes further than simply refraining from violent actions. It denotes not doing harm of any kind, across the board, and is in fact sometimes translated non-harming. As expressed in the Shandilya Upanishad, "Ahimsa is not causing pain to any living being at any time through the actions of one's mind, speech or body." Note the inclusion of mind and speech; as we've all experienced, we can cause harm not only through physical actions, but also with words, body language, and even thought. And we're karmically responsible whether the damage we do is experienced by the victim physically, mentally, emotionally, or all of the above.

Simply put, ahimsa extends the famous Hippocratic Oath, "First, do no harm," beyond medical ethics to a universal value: don't do harm to others—and "others," according to some commentators, includes sentient beings who don't happen to be human. In a sense, all other virtues are subsumed by this simple adage, since the underlying purpose of every ethical standard is to avert avoidable injury, pain, or suffering. As for the payoff, the Yoga Sutras (2, 35) promises nothing less than this: "In the presence of one firmly established in nonviolence, all hostilities cease." Another translation expresses it this way: "When a man becomes steadfast in his abstention from harming others, then all living creatures will cease to feel enmity in his presence."

I've met spiritual aspirants from a variety of paths who regard ahimsa as their lodestar. Even if they've never heard the Sanskrit term, nonviolence is the light by which they steer their way through life, the standard by which they gauge their moral and spiritual development. It could be said that one of modern history's premiere social warriors was one of them. Mahatma Gandhi put ahimsa on the map—principally the map of India, as his nonviolent movement rid the nation of its British overlords, but also the American civil rights movement and freedom campaigns around the world. Gandhi made famous the phrase *ahimsa paramo dharma*, which dates back to the Mahabharata. It means, depending on how one translates the word dharma, "non-violence is the greatest good/virtue/duty/responsibility."

Practicing ahimsa does not require extreme austerity, like that observed by Jain ascetics who wear cloth masks to prevent themselves from harming tiny organisms by breathing them in, and who sweep the ground ahead of them when they walk so as not to step on a living insect. Nor should it be taken as an absolute without regard to real-life complexities. As mentioned earlier, virtually every legal and religious prohibition against killing makes exceptions for self-defense and morally justified combat. "Circumstances arise when it is right and proper to arm oneself in defence of one's country and slay aggressive invaders, or when it is ethically correct to destroy a murderous assailant," wrote the philosopher Paul Brunton in a treatise on karma. "What must always be avoided is the infliction of unnecessary pain."[47]

Most of the world recognizes this distinction. Judicial systems commonly distinguish among first degree murder, involuntary manslaughter, negligent homicide, and other variations of killing, and prescribe different punishments for assault depending on the perpetrator's intent and method. Presumably, the laws of karma are similarly judicious.

Just as healthcare practitioners sometimes need to inflict pain—anything from a routine injection to chemotherapy—in order to avert far greater pain, there are times when some amount of harm is a side effect of preventing greater harm to greater numbers of people. The Bhagavad Gita centers on just such nuance. The inciting incident finds the esteemed warrior Arjuna at a crossroads, torn between conflicting duties. On the one hand, he is unequivocally responsible for protecting his people, who are under threat from evil forces. On the other hand, he is duty-bound by custom to do no harm to his relatives, and the bad guys on the other side of the battlefield happen to include his cousins and uncles. His adviser—no less than Lord Krishna, a divine incarnation and therefore the voice of cosmic wisdom—tells him that, under the circumstances, the greater good is to fight. He tells him a whole lot more, as we'll see in chapter 7, but the point here is that even in far simpler times, when norms and duties were clearly spelled out, determining the right thing to do was not always clear cut. How much more so in today's knotty world? And Arjuna's dilemma is just a tiny sliver of the epic Mahabharata, which for centuries has been teaching lessons about virtue in the context of a long, bloody war. The Bible does the same, as do many novels, films, plays, and operas.

Life is complicated. So is karma. So is ahimsa. Circumstances matter. Once, while driving on a city street, I ran into a ten-year-old boy who had dashed between two parked cars in pursuit of a ball. It wasn't my fault, but the people rushing to the boy's aide didn't know that. I saw menace in their eyes. For a brief moment, I thought of stepping on the gas and getting the hell out of there. But conscience intervened. I pulled over and helped carry the child to a safe spot. His leg was broken. I explained what happened to the others, and soon to the police, greatly relieved that an eyewitness corroborated my account. I was so moved by the child's pain and his family's anguish that I followed the ambulance to the emergency room to see if I could help. I didn't know the word karma at the time, but I like to think that by acting responsibly I compensated for any debt I'd incurred if, for example, I'd been driving a bit too fast or had been too slow to hit the brake. Certainly, the same accident would have produced a far different karmic scenario if I'd been drinking, or texting, or screaming at the radio over a news report. And surely, had I indulged that initial impulse to flee the scene, the karmic debt would have been heavy.

We do harm to one another all the time. But karma is conditional. Accidents are scored differently than the same act done deliberately and with malice. Firing a gun at a person out of tribal hatred or bigotry is different from shooting the same person because he's about to detonate a bomb. Scolding a child to protect her and teach her a valuable lesson is obviously different from yelling out of anger, cruelty, or selfishness, even if the child's tears are the same in both instances.

Ahimsa is perhaps the best example of a point we'll dive into in a later chapter: outer behavior is a reflection of our inner state. Recognizing what the least harmful course of action is at any given moment, and then following through, is a whole lot easier, and a great deal more natural, when we're sensitive to the needs of others, when we feel connected to them, when we're able to anticipate the impact of our actions, when we're calm and content and in an unselfish frame of mind with our hearts open to compassion. Absent those conditions, we're far more likely to do harm whether we want to or not.

Satya

The word means non-falsehood. In the vernacular, "Don't lie." In Bob Dylanese, "Let us not talk falsely now, the hour is getting late." Or, if you prefer the positive slant, "Speak the truth."

The harm done by falsehood, whether out of good intentions gone awry, or careless disregard, or deliberate deception, is potentially so destructive that it is universally condemned by religious and secular lawgivers alike. One component of Buddha's Eightfold Path is right speech. One of the Ten Commandments is "You shall not bear false witness." Hinduism's Mahanirvana Tantra combines the do and the don't: "No virtue is more excellent than truthfulness, no sin greater than lying.[48] By implication, speech that is both false and cruel would produce a megadose of negative karma, which is why, watching the public pronouncements of certain politicians, I sometimes fear for America's collective karma.

But once again there are nuances to sort out and exceptions to be made. We all know that truthful speech can do harm when misdirected or spoken with malice. It can reasonably be assumed that the karmic benefits of satya would not apply to the kind of truth telling we call brutally honest, let alone in-your-face "Let me tell you what I really think of you" eruptions that lead to feuds, grudges, and fistfights. That's probably why the Bhagavad Gita's verse about "the discipline of speech" (17:15) adds other standards to the truth component: "words that do not cause distress, that are truthful, pleasant, and beneficial." Essentially, we are advised to be honest but kind, to speak the truth with consideration for those who will be affected by what we say.

We are further advised, when faced with a choice of telling a truth that might cause harm or telling a lie to protect another's feelings, that it's best to say nothing at all. But, as we know, that's not always possible. Do you tell your best friend that her spouse is having an affair? Do you tell your adopted child his real parents are serving life sentences? Would it be kind of a doctor to tell a patient there's a fifty percent chance their condition is terminal, or would the impact of hearing that be worse than remaining ignorant? And what of circumstances where telling a lie might facilitate an act of kindness? While working on this section, I had the good karma of encountering an online talk by a swami named Nirviseshananda Tirtha,[49] who told a story about the nineteenth-century Indian educator Ishwar Chandra Vidyasagar. When a close friend of his died, leaving his widow unable to provide for her children, Vidyasagar wanted to help. Knowing that the widow was too proud to accept handouts, he uncharacteristically spoke an untruth. He said he'd borrowed money from her late husband and was unable to pay it back in full, offering instead to make monthly payments so he could discharge his debt honorably. Who would argue that the intent of the lie was not altruistic?

Some commentators have broadened the meaning of satya beyond the category of ordinary speech. They implore us, for the sake of communal harmony and our own karma, not to defraud, not to engage in duplicity, not to be deceptive, and not to indulge in rumor mongering and idle gossip. Some apply satya even more broadly: dedicating ourselves to the search for the truth at every level of concern; being able to tell the truth about our mistakes; avoiding self-deception by being utterly honest in our self-assessments. Simply put, we're to act with integrity. We're to be trustworthy. We're to honor the truth and eschew falsehood in all arenas of behavior.

In the end, when faced with uncertainty about satya in any given circumstance, the wise choice is to circle back to ahimsa: what will cause the least harm? Karmically speaking, it's crucial to weigh our options with a genuine intent to serve the highest good.

Asteya

This one sounds simple. *Asteya* means nonstealing. Hands off the merchandise! More politely, do not take anything of value from another person without authorization or permission—not even by borrowing something and neglecting to return it. Don't take what doesn't belong to you is as universal as a behavioral injunction can get.

But asteya can also be applied to nonmaterial items. What about appropriating someone else's idea and profiting from it? That might be harmless in some instances, but in others it might deprive the originator of income or reputation. What about usurping someone's time? Is that a form of stealing? Dominating someone's attention? Sapping their energy? Asking for favors and not reciprocating? Are you stealing from your employer or from your coworkers if you take the time to do something personal when you're supposed to be working? Is bending the truth on your tax return both a violation of satya and a form of stealing from the public coffers, or is it karmically inconsequential because everyone does it? Are those who are privileged enough to live in an affluent country with cheap energy and abundant consumer goods stealing precious resources from other cultures?

Once again, we're reminded that we can't be absolutist about moral precepts when pondering the imponderables of karma. What if, for example, petty shoplifting is the only thing that stands between a parent feeding a child or letting it go hungry? If you secretly confiscate someone's car keys to keep him from driving drunk, is that theft? What about a government that raises taxes on the wealthy to provide for the poor? There's a reason we see Robin Hood as a hero, not as a common thief.

Finally, some spiritual teachings take asteya to a level that might be worth contemplating. In the Swami Prabhavananda-Christopher Isherwood commentary on the Yoga Sutras, we're urged to adopt the attitude that we are guests on the planet, and nothing really belongs to us. "At best, we are merely borrowers," they say, and we should "borrow no more from the world than we absolutely need, and to make full and proper use of it." Ah, but we in the affluent West feel that we *need* refrigerators and cars and televisions and air-conditioners and, of course, smartphones. Are we borrowing too much from the many who need food, toilets, and clean water?

I'm reminded of a story about a nineteenth-century rabbi who was so revered that pilgrims came from far and wide just to lay eyes on him. One visitor was shocked to see that the rabbi's home was a small room with only a bed, a chair, and a table. "Where is your furniture?" the visitor asked.

"Where is yours?" the rabbi replied.

"But I'm just a visitor here."

"So am I," said the rabbi.

It might be karmically helpful to hold the spirit of "I'm just a visitor here" in mind, even if it's unlikely we can fully live up to it. Even cave-dwellers can be challenged to meet that standard. Once, at a massive religious festival in India called a Kumbh Mela, a brawl erupted between two bands of naked *sadhus* (ascetics) who had left their remote caves just for the holy occasion. They were fighting over which group was entitled to bathe at the confluence of sacred rivers at the most auspicious time.

Brahmacharya

Brahmacharya is usually equated with celibacy. It's synonymous with the first stage of Hindu life, when one is meant to focus on study and prepare for adulthood. It is also the name given to the first stage of monastic vows. It implies complete abstention from sex for the purpose of channeling sexual energy upward to activate higher states of consciousness. Scholars have suggested that this austere interpretation of brahmacharya made the cut because Patanjali was addressing monks.

For the vast majority of humankind who are not monastically inclined, the yama of brahmacharya is interpreted more liberally. Strictly speaking, the word means behavior, conduct, or comportment (*charya*) worthy of Brahma, which could refer either to Brahman, the ultimate reality, or Brahma, the creator deity, or brahmin, the *varna* (aka caste) responsible for preserving and disseminating sacred teachings. Hence, one common interpretation: conduct conducive to the pursuit of wisdom and spiritual liberation.

It should be emphasized that the Hindu tradition describes four principal aims or objectives for householders, i.e., everyone except monks and nuns. Known collectively as the *purusharthas,* the four are: *moksha,* spiritual liberation (the overarching goal shared by householders and renunciates); *dharma,* which has multiple meanings, as we've seen, but can roughly be thought of as behaving righteously and in accord with one's responsibilities to society; *artha,* prosperity; and *kama,* pleasure. Yes, contrary to the ascetic image of the Indic spiritual traditions, worldly delights are valued, and that includes sensory pleasure, as evidenced by the famous *Kama Sutra*, which might be loosely translated as Pleasure Manual.

And so, for non-renunciates, brahmacharya typically takes on the meaning of self-control or self-restraint. The implication is, don't over-indulge sexually; don't overwork the senses; enjoy pleasure, but without attachment, without obsession, and without overshadowing the higher aims of life. At the same time, a balanced view would suggest that we also avoid the other extreme, suppression. Being mentally obsessed by feelings we're trying hard to shoo away might be more distracting than responsibly yielding to those urges. Psychologists would add that suppression can lead to all manner of neuroses and can wreak havoc with the body and nervous system.

I'm reminded of the Buddhist story of two monks walking through the countryside on pilgrimage. They come to a river and prepare to wade across it when a young woman appears. She needs to get to the other side of the river, but she is small of stature and fears that the water is too deep and the current too strong. So, the senior monk picks her up and carries her to the far shore. The monks resume their trek. After a while, the junior monk gets up the nerve to question the other's behavior: "We took a vow never to touch a woman, yet you lifted one in your arms and held her close to your body."

The senior monk replies, "I left the woman at the riverbank, but you're still carrying her."

Redefining brahmacharya for non-monastic moderns would seem to call for a sense of balance that resonates with Buddha's Middle Way and this verse from the Bhagavad Gita (6: 16-17): "Yoga is not for those who eat too much or those who do not eat at all. Nor is it for they who sleep too much or those who stay awake." Contemporary spiritual teacher Acharya Shunya, the first female head of a venerable Vedic lineage, claims that the ancient seers did not intend to prohibit sex among householders, but were concerned with the "what, when, where, how much, with whom." In that context, she suggests this interpretation: "choosing a balanced and healthy expression of sexuality between committed partners."

One more consideration. Some commentators have updated brahmacharya to embrace the ethic of not abusing or exploiting anyone sexually. This not only makes good moral sense, but it's also consistent with the concept of brahmacharya as restraint, control, and moderation. If one's appetites are under control, meaning not compulsive or obsessive, they are less likely to lead to harmful behavior.

Aparigraha

This yama takes nonstealing to another level: Don't even think about it. The word *graha* means to take, to seize, or grab. *Pari* means "on all sides." And the prefix "a" turns any word into its negative form as "non" (e.g., *himsa* = *harm*, *ahimsa* = nonharming). Taken together, aparigraha implies not trying to possess more than you need, or not pining for what isn't necessary. Hence, the most frequent translation: noncoveting. This brings to mind the last of the Ten Commandments: "You shall not covet your neighbor's house. You shall not covet your neighbor's wife, or his male or female servant, his ox or donkey, or anything that belongs to your neighbor."

Other translations of aparigraha include qualities such as non-attachment, non-possessiveness, non-greed, and "nonacceptance of gifts." The last item might be a hard sell in the modern West, where gift-giving is a virtue, if not an obligation, and turning down a gift is considered rude, if not a relationship-ender. In the context in which the Yoga Sutras were composed, however, it might have made sense. Feuerstein notes that yogis were "encouraged to cultivate voluntary simplicity" because possessions lead to attachment, fear of loss, and mental distraction. It's a sentiment that many spiritual seekers can relate to in a culture where the things we own tend to own us. In a sense, like brahmacharya, aparigraha directs us away from unwise energy expenditure, freeing that energy for higher, more spiritual pursuits. It's also a deterrent to Shakespeare's "green-eyed monster," envy, and we all know what envy can make us do.

Perhaps a modern version of aparigraha might be something like: Be prosperous and comfortable, but don't get attached to unnecessary possessions; don't get greedy; don't accumulate for egoic reasons; don't strive to get something for nothing; don't feed the green-eyed monster. Perhaps the karmically beneficial approach is to live well but simply, and to be grateful for what we have. It would also behoove us to discern the difference between wanting things that offer comfort and pleasure and giving in to a feverish desire for stuff that might, in the larger scope of things, be wasteful and burdensome.

The Buddhist precept of right livelihood enters in as well. We spend a major portion of our waking hours earning our livings, so *how* we do it can have major karmic consequences. Working for a tobacco company or a manufacturer that pollutes the air and water is different from doing the same job for a nonprofit health provider or a group that feeds the homeless. And, needless to say, it would not be good karma to achieve material success while exploiting employees or deceiving customers.

Other Precepts

It should be noted that the five yamas are identical to the five main householder vows (*vratas*) in the Jain tradition. They are also congruent with core ethical injunctions for Buddhist laypersons, the best-known iteration of which is the Five Precepts: not killing, not stealing, not misusing sex (sometimes translated "not desiring in excess"), not lying, not abusing intoxicants.

To which some Buddhists add these five.

Not criticizing others. The intent seems to be twofold: prevent interpersonal disharmony and protect individuals from the karmic consequences of mean-spirited speech. The precept is echoed in the sacred texts of Hinduism, where those who don't speak ill of others are rewarded, and in the New Testament where Jesus says, "Do not judge, or you too will be judged," and "Why do you look at the speck of sawdust in your brother's eye and pay no attention to the plank in your own eye?" (Matthew 7:1–4).

Not elevating oneself over others. Curb that runaway ego! Bragging, insulting, and trying to make oneself look tall by figuratively beheading others is not good karma—at least in the long run, since such behavior can appear to yield short-term dividends.

Not being stingy. This is implied in asteya, nonstealing, and it's in sync with directives about generosity and charity found in all traditions. If karmic law is consistent, stingy people would find that others are not as generous with them as they'd like them to be.

Not being angry. We all know what can happen when we're enraged: misguided words, regrettable deeds, irreparable feuds, and even violence. The Bhagavad Gita (2:63) puts it this way: "From anger comes delusion; from delusion, disturbed memory; from disturbed memory, the loss of discernment; from loss of discernment, the life is wasted." But isn't anger sometimes justified? Doesn't it often spur remedial action? Of course, but there's a big difference between the unconstrained fury of rage and the controlled, strategic strength of righteous indignation.

Not speaking ill of the Three Treasures. Those Treasures (aka Gems, Jewels, or Refuges) are: the Buddha (not just the historic Buddha, but all the wise ones who guide seekers to liberation), the Dharma (in the Buddhist context, the body of teachings), and the Sangha (the spiritual community). This precept may have been intended for the karmic protection of the Buddhist collective, but it can be applied to any spiritual seeker at any time: treat your teachers with respect; approach sacred teachings with reverence; cherish the spiritual assemblies in which you participate.

We might have to modify the bit about not speaking ill of them in our day and age, in light of the scandals that have afflicted spiritual leaders and institutions. The Dalai Lama himself has advised Buddhists to speak out if they get wind of improper behavior. Surely there's a distinction to be made between being truthful and being malicious; between speaking out to protect others from harm and stirring up fear and anger without merit; between calling out problems to improve an organization and lashing out to destroy it. It should be noted that, in other Buddhist texts, slander and vain or frivolous chatter are considered just as harmful as lying.

Further Reflections on Don'ts

It's helpful to keep in mind that all the precepts and guidelines are deeply interrelated. An improvement in one will have a positive impact on our ability to act in accord with the others. Similarly, coming up short on one can reverberate to the others in varying degrees. Take aparigraha as a starter. Let's say you covet wealth. That can lead to compromises in asteya—if not outright stealing, then perhaps an attempt to take advantage of others or to not honor an agreement. You might be tempted to conceal, mislead, or otherwise take liberties with the truth, thus failing to meet the satya standard. And, as we've seen in both news reports and fiction, the hunger for wealth can lead to the antithesis of brahmacharya, whether you interpret it as abstinence, moderation, or ethically responsible sex. Any or all of which can cause harm. Bottom line: not abiding by one precept can trouble the karmic waters in other ways as well.

Wings of desire

Being unable to refrain from doing something we know we shouldn't do often comes down to the streetcar named desire running through all the stop signs. Whether the carrot dangling before us is fame, wealth, power, sex, or any other target of lust, desire can overpower reason, good sense, and noble intentions. It can bury our ethical standards and ultimately lead to harm, both to others and ourselves. That's why the Eastern traditions flash warning signs about desire. The satisfaction of fulfilling a desire, they teach, is invariably short-lived, at which point a new one steps into line. In the classic cycle, desire leads to actions aimed at fulfilling the desire; the actions create impressions in the mind; those impressions lead to other desires, which lead to actions, and on and on. All of which has karmic consequences.

Unfortunately, this reasonable analysis of the nature of desire has sometimes been taken to an extreme, leading to a demonization of desire *as such*. Desire has been portrayed as the chief obstacle to spiritual liberation, an assertion that has led to misguided attempts to destroy all traces of desire. Which, ironically, has led to all manner of misery. Treating desire itself as a spiritual obstacle invariably triggers suppression, unnatural behavior, and the denial of our humanness.

Let's stipulate that desire is as unkillable as a vampire. As long as we inhabit human bodies we'll have desires. At the very least, we'll want food to eat and water to drink, clothing to wear and shelter from the cold and heat. Once, in India, I wandered into an abandoned ashram and met the one swami still living there. He was old, and he lived in a tiny hut with a thin sleeping mat, a rickety table, and a rudimentary cooking stove. When I saw him the first time, he was hanging his one spare orange garment on a clothesline while singing a Sanskrit chant with Broadway musical exuberance. We chatted a while, and I left thinking I'd been privileged to meet the most desireless, supremely content human being I'd ever encountered.

The next day I went back to see him, bringing two bananas and a papaya as a kind of offering. At one point, I asked what he thought about all day. He chuckled at the question. I followed up with, "Do you think about God?"

"I used to think about God," he replied. "Now God thinks about me."

I gave him a look that said, essentially, "What the hell does that mean?"

He explained, by way of an example, that he'd realized that morning that he was out of provisions and would have to walk into town in hopes that someone would give him food. In his order of swamis, it was not permitted to carry money or to ask for anything. The Indian people know this and consider it good karma to give ascetics what they need. But my new friend had diabetes, and his feet hurt, so he thought he would have to go without food. "And you came with banana and papaya," he said. "God was thinking about me."

It was an unforgettable experience, and a great lesson. The swami had practically nothing, but he was utterly certain that the universe would provide. At the same time, it's undeniable that he *desired* food, or at least acknowledged the need for it. And surely, there were times when he desired wood for his fire, a new jug for his water, and maybe a new orange shawl.

The point is, if even hard-core yogis have bodily needs that translate to desire, what of the rest of us? Is it undesirable to desire creature comforts? What about the desire to provide for our children? To help make our loved ones happy? To do what we can to cool off the planet and bring about social justice? We can only conclude that desire is not only inevitable, it's not all bad. And even if all desires *were* spiritually detrimental, what would we do about the desire to not have desires?

The task before us is not to vanquish desire, which would be futile, but to keep desire from sparking actions that lead to piles of karmic debt. That means managing our desires wisely: to desire the right things in the right way; to shift as best we can from lower, selfish desires to higher, nobler, karmically beneficial ones attuned to the greater good; and to modulate the intensity of desire, lowering the flame from a frenzied boil to a nice, even simmer, from desperate grasping to unattached preference, from "gotta have it" to "it would be nice to have."

Something else to be vigilant about: the tendency to create a permission structure for doing things we'd be better off avoiding. The ego is a trickster; it can persuade the mind to serve its selfish aims and defy the soul's better intentions. How many times have you found a way to justify doing something that your better angels knew was merely ego-puffing, only to regret it later on? We can easily convince ourselves that an action we feel compelled to take will not only accrue to our short-term satisfaction but benefit others as well, and maybe even have cosmic significance. I've actually heard statements like this: "On the surface this might appear to be wrong, but from the God's-eye-view it's perfect and the karmic rewards will be great." That kind of mental trickery is why it's a good idea to keep in mind this simple formula from Swami Medhananda of the Vedanta Society: "Do that which makes you less selfish and less egoistic, and don't do that which makes you more selfish and egoistic."

Strong emotions and feverish desires can even make disreputable actions seem heroic. Take revenge, for example. How many movie heroes have been motivated by the desire to get even? We cheer for the likes of Liam Neeson as they hunt down the bad guys, and we root for them to vanquish the foe in the final confrontation. Revenge is extremely satisfying, whether served cold or hot. But is it good karma? Only occasional works of genius, like Shakespeare's *Othello*, address the complexities lurking in the shadows of revenge.

Once there was a noble samurai whose beloved master was murdered. The grief-stricken warrior knows he is duty-bound to avenge the crime. He travels far afield under arduous conditions in search of the killer and finally comes across him in an encampment. His prey is a sitting duck. The samurai can do away with him with one swipe of his mighty sword. He tiptoes close enough to do the deed. The killer sees him, realizes what is about to happen, and spits at the samurai in contempt. Enraged by that gesture, the samurai raises the sword above his head ... and stops. Why? Because, while the code he lives by compels him to deliver the punishment, it also forbids him from striking a foe in a state of anger. So he scurries away, vowing to do his duty after he gets his wrath under control.

Forgive those trespassers

One intervention we might do when we're feeling resentful or consumed by a desire to retaliate is to remind ourselves that while the target of our grievance may indeed have done something awful, he or she is also delivering our own package of karma—and we are now positioned to return the favor. We can rationalize an act of revenge—"Hey, I'm just an instrument for their karma, enabling them to reap what they sowed"—but we should also understand that whatever we choose to do will create a new chain of karma. Thinking ahead, therefore, acting in accord with ahimsa might be a better way to balance the books. As Gandhi famously said, "An eye for an eye makes the whole world blind."

Think of Nelson Mandela and Archbishop Desmond Tutu when South Africa finally put an end to apartheid. Instead of giving license to victims to lash out in rage, however much it would have been justified, they calmed the waters by establishing the Truth and Reconciliation Commission. The purpose, in the words of a South African official at the time, was "to enable South Africans to come to terms with their past on a morally accepted basis and to advance the cause of reconciliation."

Since many of our most regrettable acts are triggered by feeling disappointed, betrayed, wounded, insulted, or abused by other people, it follows that forgiveness would be an effective preventive measure—a stop sign on the road to ruinous behavior. Logic suggests that, done with sincerity, forgiving would redirect the karmic current in a more positive direction. In fact, what religions have long suggested about the healing power of forgiveness has to some degree been validated by science. An article on the National Institutes of Health website reports that "Empirical studies have shown that forgiveness decreases anger, anxiety, and depression and increases self-esteem and hopefulness for the future."[50] By contrast, according to studies analyzed at the Johns Hopkins Medicine website, "People who hang on to grudges … are more likely to experience severe depression and post-traumatic stress disorder, as well as other health conditions."[51]

In recent years, psychologists have proffered a good deal of advice about how to go about forgiving without being taken advantage of. Here are some key points: 1) Forgiving doesn't mean abandoning self-protection or making yourself vulnerable to further abuse, 2) it's not like issuing a pardon or a get out of jail free card; you can still hold people accountable, 3) forgiveness is not for the other person; it's for your own well-being, 4) it's internally transformative; those who work authentically to forgive typically feel liberated from the emotional weight of carrying a grudge, and freed from the compulsive behavior that stored-up anger can lead to. As Jack Kornfield notes, "Forgiveness is the heart's capacity to release its grasp on the pains of the past and free itself to go on." In fact, the person you forgive doesn't even have to know about it.

Sowing seeds of forgiveness might be harder than exacting revenge, but forgivers reap sweeter karmic fruits than the vengeful. When you find yourself resisting the wisdom of forgiveness because it seems like avoidance, it might help to remember something Gandhi said: "The weak can never forgive. Forgiveness is the attribute of the strong."

Forgiveness begins at home

As many of us have discovered and researchers have confirmed, sometimes the hardest person to forgive is oneself. Anyone with a conscience will feel what a friend of mine called "the slow acid drip of regret" when they misbehave. But self-forgiveness is critical for anyone who believes, or even suspects, that karma is real. It's a form of the radical acceptance we discussed earlier, a necessary adaptation to a world run by karmic law. It means accepting who we are in spite of our limitations. It means facing up to the obvious fact that we're bound to screw up; we won't always do the right thing, and sometimes we'll do the wrong thing either intentionally or inadvertently. At times, we'll get confused and freeze in place like Arjuna, not knowing which fork in the road to take, and we won't have a divine incarnation to guide us; at best, we'll have an internal Yogi Berra saying, "When you come to a fork in the road, take it," and we'll just have to buckle up, maybe flip a coin, and do our best.

Sometimes our egos will overrule our judgment. Our intellect will align with our lower urges and deceive us. Habits we thought we'd kicked, and behavior patterns we thought we'd left in the wretched past, will resurface. "I can't tell you how many times I've sworn to never again get defensive when my wife criticizes me," a friend of mine recently said. To which his wife added, "And I can't tell you how many times I've vowed to stop being judgmental." But the spouses know that, for better and for worse, the karmic matchmaker coupled them in this life so they can learn and grow together. They take that assignment seriously, even if they sometimes get impatient with what seems like a glacial rate of progress. But they have indeed progressed. Early on, before they viewed their marriage as a learning environment, they would not have laughed about their challenges, as they did when talking to me.

When we've made yet another mistake, we need to remember that what we do while waiting for the karma to bounce back to us will affect our future. We can flagellate ourselves or we can forgive ourselves. Sure, a certain amount of self-scolding might be a useful way to drive home a lesson and add strength to a commitment to change. But karmic law doesn't operate like religious codes, with severe punishment and threats of eternal damnation for so-called sinners. Personal karma is modifiable. As we've seen, this suggests that mistakes are best treated as learning opportunities, with kindness, patience, clarity, determination, and yes, forgiveness. That doesn't mean making excuses or finding ways to justify what we've done, but rather taking full responsibility, holding ourselves accountable, accepting, even loving, our blundering selves and resolving sincerely to do better next time.

Amends can mend

You may remember the catchphrase—what we now might call a meme—"Love means never having to say you're sorry." It was spawned by a sappy romantic novel called *Love Story* by Erich Segal, and the movie version with Ali MacGraw and Ryan O'Neal. Well, a lot of couples have laughed at that line and turned it into "Marriage means *always* having to say you're sorry." Less cynically, we could say that being human means sometimes having to say you're sorry. If you care about your karma, apologizing helps, *if the apology is heartfelt.* Even more helpful is to put your words into action.

That might explain why the eighth and ninth steps in Twelve Steps programs have proved essential in overcoming the karma of addiction. Step 8 is, "Made a list of all the persons we had harmed and became willing to make amends to them all." Step 9: "Made direct amends to such people wherever possible, except when to do so would injure them or others."

In other words, don't just send a text saying "I apologize" with a heart emoji, and don't just toss off "I'm sorry" over drinks and change the subject. Chances are, karmic law is friendlier to those who walk the talk, willingly and earnestly.

How exactly should we make amends? Psychologist David Hawkins, the director of the Marriage Recovery Center, suggests these three steps:

1. "A sincere expression of *remorse* is a simple statement that you are truly sorry for what you've done without excuses, dismissal, and rationalizations."
2. "A statement of *responsibility*. We accept and understand our behavior's impact on the injured party."

3. "*Restitution.* We are willing to take whatever steps are necessary to make it up to the injured person—to listen to what they need from us."[52]

Making amends is an act of restoration, a way to repair something that was broken and to make things right. It's healing for both the wounded and the wounder. At its best, it reinforces the karmic importance of acting differently in the future.

Closely related to making amends is the tradition of doing penance. This isn't everyone's cup of tea, but for those with strong ties to a religion it can be profoundly meaningful. That's why every tradition has ways of making up for wrong behavior and, in theistic religions, letting God know we're sorry, expressing remorse, and vowing to do better. In some cases, it can also mean praying to be forgiven. What's called penance might entail anything from making a financial contribution to acts of service such as helping the needy to performing a prescribed ritual such as going to confession, making offerings, or circumnavigating a shrine a set number of times. The logic of karma suggests that, religious beliefs aside, penance would be effective only in proportion to the contrition, humility, and sincerity with which it is performed.

Bottom Lines

It's hard to imagine anyone having read this and the previous chapter carefully unless they really want to do the right thing and not do the wrong thing. If you're among those who truly want to give it a go, you probably already know that it's not necessarily easy. You may have made efforts before and fallen short. But the very fact that you *want* to stop doing karmically harmful things is no doubt a sign that the karma that led to past mistakes is weakening. You're getting sick of it, like a longtime smoker who can no longer stand the taste of burning tobacco and is fed up with the smoke in their eyes, the coughing, and the social disapproval, not to mention the burden of knowing that health consequences are on the way. It's just that the next step, the final transformation, can be tough.

Sometimes, however, when you're really ready for change, it can be surprisingly easy. I tried for a couple years to stop smoking. I cut down to two or three cigarettes a day and whipped myself every night over my failure to take the necessary final step. Then one day, I smoked a cigarette and knew it was my last one. And it was.

If your karma has brought you to a place where you're ready to upgrade your future karma, you might need nothing more intricate than the Bob Newhart formula: Stop it!

If you prefer a hipper inspiration, take it from Miles Davis. At one point in his legendary career, the trumpeter and band leader hired a young genius saxophonist for his quintet. The newcomer, John Coltrane, would take off on solos that were as long and unpredictable as they were brilliant. This did not suit the disciplined Davis, but Coltrane couldn't bring the solos down to a suitable length. He said he got carried away, captivated by the sound and the process, and time disappeared. The frustrated Davis reportedly said, "Just put down the horn, man."

And there you have it: "Just do no harm."

6

What Are You Thinking?

The Power of Thoughts and Intentions

"Karma is thought as much as action, desire as much as deed. The one is the seed which fructifies into the other and cannot be separated from it."
—*Paul Brunton*

An acquaintance I'll call Henry confessed to me that he was thinking of having an affair. He was about fifty years old then and had been married for close to twenty years to an accomplished, loyal, and thoroughly decent woman. Together, they had raised two children, who were twelve and fifteen at the time. He'd already had one affair that I knew of. It had occurred nine years earlier and had come close to ending his marriage before he came to his senses and returned to his family. Luckily for Henry, his wife was able to forgive, although she certainly did not forget.

Now, whether by chance or a confluence of karmic events, he'd run into an ex-girlfriend. In their twenties they'd had the kind of intense relationship that goes down in flames but is never entirely extinguished. For Henry, it lived on in deep impressions, romanticized memories, and the occasional "what-if" and "whatever happened to" rumination. When he ran into the ex, he immediately felt a stirring of the old passion, and he was sure that she felt it too. It made him realize that, for all the cozy joys of family life, his marriage lacked excitement. He missed the energy of pure lust, and the possibility of turning up the heat was so intoxicating that he couldn't stop thinking about it. "Why not get it out of my system for good with one last fling?" he said. "She and I obviously have some unfinished karma."

He acknowledged that there could be unintended consequences, but he thought the chances of his wife finding out were slim since the ex was also married and was in town for only a few days.

In the end, it was the woman, not Henry, who turned away from the abyss. But the incident illustrates a few things about karma that I shared with Henry and will repeat here.

First, as the story illustrates, our actions are always preceded by thought—not necessarily coherent, rational thought with the kind of analysis Henry was attempting, but some form of mental activity, however momentary and inchoate. As Swami Vivekananda put it over a century ago, "All the actions that we see in the world, all the movements in human society, all the works that we have around us, are simply the display of thought, the manifestation of the will of man."

Our interaction with the environment resonates with impressions baked into the nervous system, and as a result, thought impulses arise. This is true even of acts that take place so quickly they appear to have no mental antecedent. We swat away a fly. We slam on the brakes when a car cuts us off. We take a child in our arms when she cries. We tense up when a figure appears in the dark. We call such actions instinctive, and they certainly seem to be unconscious, but it's safe to assume that something transpires in the mind between stimulus and response.

A second, more subtle point, is that our thoughts, *in and of themselves,* produce karma. Thought is a form of energy, and it's reasonable to assume that the energy does not remain within the confines of our skulls but instead vibrates outward to produce karmic consequences for better and for worse. Henry's cogitation about whether to ignite the affair; his obsessive chewing on whether a fling would put an end to future temptations or make them more likely; the lurid fantasizing about the delights he would enjoy—all of that was karmically significant. His thoughts were already affecting his life and his marriage regardless of what would eventually occur.

Readers of a certain age will remember when, in 1976, then-presidential candidate Jimmy Carter told a *Playboy* interviewer, "I've committed adultery in my heart many times." Citing the New Testament (Matthew 5:27-28), the pious Carter said that Jesus looked upon sinful thoughts as the equivalent of the act itself, and because he (Carter) had "looked on many women with lust," he could not judge anyone who "screws lots of women." It was a small passage in a long, substantive interview, but historians say it came close to costing Carter the election. He and his wife, Rosalynn, were hounded about the statement and he was widely mocked as a religious nut.

Still, maybe Carter was on to something. If you set aside the theology of a deity who spies on everyone's thoughts like a computer hacker and recast his statement in karmic language, you come to a profound concept: what we think and feel has a bigger causal impact than we realize. This leads us to conclude that adhering to codes of conduct can take us only so far. If we want to restructure our karmic accounts we also have to attend to the internal domains that give rise to everything we say and do on the physical plane. We'll begin that process here and continue to a deeper level in the following chapter.

Layer Upon Layer

India's sages investigated the inner dimensions of human existence with the rigor of scientists, and in the process discovered hierarchical layers, much as their Western counterparts unearthed molecules, atoms, and subatomic particles beneath the surface of material objects.

The yogis discerned five sheaths, called *koshas*, which nest like Russian dolls, one inside the other, surrounding the eternal, formless Atman that is the ultimate Self. (Buddhists also speak of the koshas, but reject the notion of a permanent self.) Unlike solid dolls, but very much like the energy layers described by physics, the qualities of the *panchakoshas* (pancha means five) change progressively from the outside in, moving from the gross to the subtle and the tangible to the intangible, with each successive level having greater potential power. The five sheaths are as follows.

Annamaya kosha

This is the physical layer, the grossest of the koshas (*anna* = food, *maya* = made of), with the familiar organs, tissues, muscles, and the like that carry us through the material world. It's the layer we identify with until we learn that we're not just our bodies.

Pranamaya kosha

Known as the vital sheath, or the energy body, this is the domain of the primal life force called *prana*. Similar to what the Chinese call *chi*, prana is the pervasive energy that vitalizes biological systems and binds the mind to the body. It's closely associated with the breath, hence the yogic breathing practices known as pranayama.

Manomaya kosha

More subtle still is the mental sheath—"the body made of thought processes," as one translation has it. This is the realm of cognition. It's not synonymous with brain activity, which is physical and therefore part of annamaya kosha; it's contiguous with *mind*, the domain of thought and feeling. It's where we process sensory experience, remember, ponder, analyze, reason, and imagine—and where we worry, fear, and seethe; enjoy, hope, and appreciate. It's also the storehouse of past experience, where sensory input interacts with deeply etched impressions and shapes our perception and action.

Vijnanamaya kosha

The seers perceived a level of consciousness deeper and more elevated than the thought processes that take place in manomaya kosha. Often translated as "intellect," vijnanamaya kosha is where discernment, judgment, and understanding occur, and where conscience and will reside. It's the level of wisdom and direct knowing, where we separate right from wrong and take on the spiritual task of distinguishing between the infinite and the finite, the eternal and the temporal.

Anandamaya kosha

Ananda, as many readers know, means bliss. Anandamaya is, therefore, the body of bliss. It's the most subtle layer of the onion of self, and the final veil between identifying with the ego and realizing the Self as infinite. It's where diversity melts into unity. It is said that enlivening the bliss sheath is what enables us to experience love, happiness, joy, peace, contentment, and true freedom.[53]

It should be noted that anandamaya kosha is said to transcend karma entirely; those who learn to function from this level of existence are untouched by karmic law and produce no new karma of consequence.

Whether you resonate with the kosha model or an alternative, when considering karma it's of great practical significance to remember that our existence is layered and what occurs at each level affects our karmic balance sheet. A complete, holistic effort would call upon us to monitor, purify, and upgrade every layer.

Give It Another Thought

In the Yoga Sutras, just after Patanjali introduces us to the yamas and niyamas, he offers two profoundly practical verses about thought. First, chapter 2, verse 33 (Swami Satchidananda's translation): "When disturbed by negative thoughts, opposite (positive) ones should be thought of." In his translation, Swami Hariharananda Aranya expresses the same idea but refers directly to the yamas and niyamas: "When these restraints and observances are inhibited by perverse thought, the opposites should be thought of."

The sutra following that one reads (as translated by Prabhavananda and Isherwood): "The obstacles to yoga—such as acts of violence and untruth—may be directly created or indirectly caused or approved; they may be motivated by greed, anger, or self-interest; they may be small or moderate or great; but they never cease to result in pain and ignorance. One should overcome distracting thoughts by remembering this."

Taken together, the two verses tell us that, where karma is concerned, what goes on in our heads has consequences, some desirable and others not so much. To twist a well-known American meme about a city in Nevada, *What happens in the mind does not stay in the mind.* Remembering this gives us incentive to manage our minds wisely, just as knowing we'll freeze in a snowstorm gets us to put on a coat or knowing we can get a speeding ticket motivates us to ease up on the accelerator. "This is an absolute law of nature," write Prabhavananda and Isherwood. "If we could remember it always, we should learn to control our tongues and our thoughts."

The process of replacing karmically undesirable thoughts with positive alternatives is known as *pratipaksha bhavana*, pratipaksha meaning "opposite" and bhavana meaning "cultivation" (alternatively "causing to be," "producing," or "manifesting"). In other words, send in a substitute; trade in an unwanted thought for a newer, shinier model that gets better karmic mileage.

The shift from a harmful thought to a benign one is similar to the method employed by psychologists as part of cognitive behavioral therapy. Under terms such as "reframing" and "reappraisal," the basic technique has made countless appearances in self-help books and magazines going back to the 1952 megaseller by Norman Vincent Peale, *The Power of Positive Thinking*. Are you consumed by critical thoughts about someone? Think about what you admire or appreciate about them. Do you find yourself hoping that someone fails at a venture so you won't be consumed by jealousy? Send out a prayer or a wish that they succeed. Are you mentally rehearsing how to deceive someone to gain advantage? Visualize yourself being totally honest.

You don't have to believe that mind stuff vibrates outward from the brain to appreciate that both positive and negative content can impact our lives in corresponding ways. We've all seen dark rumination find its way into our moods, speech, and behavior, and we remember how that shaped our decisions, our relationships, and our well-being, i.e., our karma. And we know from experience that bright, loving states of mind have the opposite effect.

Science has, to some extent, confirmed the insights of the ancients. Studies have shown that optimism, for example, is linked to measurable outcomes such as reduced anxiety, lower rates of depression, and decreased risk of succumbing to a serious disease. One researcher, Harvard psychologist Ellen Langer, makes a commonsense argument for what she calls "mindful optimism." She writes: "One of the advantages of this approach is that it helps us focus on what we can actually control. . . . If we worry and everything turns out fine we've stressed ourselves unnecessarily. If we worry and things turn out to be bad, we're usually no more prepared for it than if we don't worry. If we relax and things turn out bad, we'll be stronger to deal with it, and if all turns out to be fine we can continue behaving adaptively."[54]

If the conclusion isn't already obvious, ask yourself this: Which is more likely to produce beneficial karma, actions that spring from appreciation and optimism or those that spew from resentment and pessimism?

The basic instruction for modifying thought patterns is simple and uncomplicated: when you notice that the contents of your mind are cruel, harsh, critical, angry, bitter, gloomy, or otherwise negative, replace them with an upbeat, elevating, harmonious equivalent. Bye bye apprehension, hello confidence; adios rage, hola acceptance; au revoir disdain, bonjour respect; ta ta despair, top of the morning hope. What could be easier, right? Well, pratipaksha bhavana can be as undemanding as tapping a toggle switch, but at other times the unwanted thought is as stubborn and clingy as a cranky toddler. That's particularly true of long-standing habits such as responding to minor disappointments with gloom and doom, or leaping from a disagreement with a loved one to fear of being abandoned, or responding to constructive criticism with an attack.

But the skill of positive replacement can be learned, and habitual negativity can be unlearned. It might not be as simple as, say, getting used to operating a toaster oven. It might be more like learning to drive a stick shift; the skill of shifting mental gears can take time to develop. With repetition, however, the ability becomes engrained, and eventually it develops into a barely conscious habit. Positive framing might even become the default setting.

Here are some tips gleaned from a variety of experts:

Monitor your mind. Start observing your mind in action on a routine basis. Become familiar with your habits and patterns. Take note of how often negativity shows up, how intense it is under various circumstances, and when it's most likely to be triggered.

Be vigilant. Stay alert for the appearance of unwanted thoughts. It can be as hard to prevent them from arising as it is to stop the rain, but we can keep an eye out for the darkening skies and be prepared to act.

Acknowledge that you have a choice. Recognize that you can choose not to get absorbed by negative energy. Then, when you notice unwanted mental content, you can do the equivalent of closing the windows or opening an umbrella.

Loosen the grip. To the extent possible, adopt the stance of neutral observer. Rather than adding fuel to the fire by ruminating, scrutinizing, arguing, or otherwise dwelling on the harmful thought stream, try to witness the procession of words and images like a spectator at a parade.

Choose the right alternative. Identifying the right replacement for an undesirable thought is not always obvious. What is the opposite of hate? It's love, right? Not so fast. Next time you're seething with hatred for someone who betrayed you, or for terrorists who committed an atrocity, or for a coworker who makes disparaging remarks, good luck replacing the hate with loving thoughts. As someone who tried it in the heat of an American election season told me, "Not even Jesus could pull off that trick." She felt like such a phony her brain rejected the intended replacement like a mismatched organ transplant.

Similar debacles occur when people choose other facile opposites. If you're gripped by a legitimate worry, for instance, inserting a rosy vision in its place might feel absurd or phony. If you're insecure about performing a task well, supreme confidence might be a bridge too far. "Positive thinking can be very effective," a cognitive psychologist told me, "but the content has to be believable." He explained that the subconscious knows what we really feel, and it has a low tolerance for platitudes and artifice. Mentally reciting "I love so-and-so" when you really can't stand so-and-so will give your subconscious a good laugh. Furthermore, the psychologist said, if your mental scenario implies taking action, the proposed action has to be feasible. Say you're uneasy about the effectiveness of your new weight-loss program. Your subconscious will greet "I'll lose fifty pounds the first week" the way it would "I'll win the Masters tournament" if you take up golf. Something believable, such as "I'll gradually lose the desired weight," would be more plausible, and therefore more effective.

In other words, when groping for an appropriate replacement thought, expand the concept of opposite. Think creatively. If your subconscious resists loving thoughts about someone you abhor, maybe settle for tolerance or indifference. Or shift your focus away from that person and instead think about someone you *do* love. It won't erase your contempt for the person who's fueling your negative thoughts, but it *will* soften your heart and shift the energy and content of your mind. Similarly, if you're condemning yourself for a mistake or a perceived failure, try conjuring memories of times when you triumphed. If you're having suspicious thoughts about someone you don't quite trust, try introducing the image of a loved one you trust implicitly, or of your children, a saint, or a favorite teacher. The point is to shift *the quality of energy*, not necessarily to literally flip the specific content.

I've spoken to people who have been quite imaginative in practicing pratipaksha bhavana. A scientist, for example, was seething with animosity for climate change deniers. She knew her concern was warranted, but she also knew the obsession wasn't doing her health or her karma any good. Since she couldn't replace her disdain with tolerance or understanding, she shifted to compassion—not for climate deniers, but for those who suffer the most from climate-related disasters—and to gratitude for those who are working tirelessly to come up with solutions.

It's important to remember that some of the thought patterns we label negative are, in fact, useful. They might be warning us of a danger. Being upset about environmental pollution is not only reasonable, it can be an impetus to constructive action. So can suspicion about a person who might cause harm. So might grief over a loss. We can go on and on with examples of thoughts that disturb, upset, or irritate but at the same time serve as warnings, teaching devices, and survival mechanisms. The key is to discern when their continued presence is karmically debilitating. At that point, creative mind shifting is called for. The wise thing to do with ferocious anger, for example, might be to replace it with a calmer and more strategically productive mindset like moral indignation. As a political activist told me, "I've learned to get past the pissed-off stage and turn it into 'That is wrong, and this is what I can do about it.'"

Fear, too, can be a healthy survival mechanism; without it we might expose ourselves to dangerous, even life-threatening, situations. At the same time, as we've all experienced, inappropriate or excessive fear can trigger a fight-flight response way out of proportion to the actual threat, creating a threat of its own, one that might imperil our health and create a new chain of karma. But trying to replace handwringing fear with bromides or feelgood gobbledygook can be an act of futility. A more effective shift from "I'm terrified" might be to something like "I'm deeply concerned" or "I'm troubled by something that needs my attention." Combine that with a compassion-driven action plan and you have a mental framework for beneficial karma.

Similarly, thoughts that reflect a sense of hopelessness and despair might be replaced by a solution-oriented thought, such as "I might be able to solve this by..." or "I can make things better by..." In such instances, the verbal thought pattern might be supplemented by visual images in which you're taking constructive action.

What if no plausible solution to a legitimate concern presents itself? Well, in that case, as wise people have always told us, fretting about it won't do any good either. Perhaps under such circumstances, worry can be replaced by a determination to search for possible solutions and ways to protect yourself and others from the worst potential outcomes. For those so inclined, an assertion of faith in the ultimate benevolence of the universe might be invoked, whether in the form of karmic law, a loving God, or another affirming precept. One solution is to replace gloom with a favorite prayer or an uplifting quotation you hold dear, something along the lines of the famous proclamation by the mystic Julian of Norwich: "All shall be well, and all shall be well, and all manner of things shall be well."

To summarize, we can shift the mind in a karmically benign direction by replacing negative thoughts with their opposites, but "opposite" can be understood in an energetic rather than a literal way. The best substitutes are believable and plausible—and the more loving, kind, and compassionate the better.

Replace the thought. Once you've selected a replacement, the next step is to make the substitution. Sometimes this is as easy as replacing a depleted battery with a new one. At other times, the unwanted thought pattern stubbornly refuses to leave, making the task more formidable—not quite a hip replacement, perhaps, but maybe like changing a tire or installing a new sink.

We've all experienced times when disturbing and debilitating thoughts race through the mind in a frenzy. We know that when those thoughts are inflamed by emotion they can run on a loop, repeating themselves like a politician on the stump. Under such stormy conditions, inserting a propitious substitute can be as hard as stopping a flood when the levee is breached. At such times, we might be tempted to try even harder—shoulder to the wheel, nose to the grindstone, and all those work ethic cliches. But force is unlikely to work, and the impulse to labor at the task can exacerbate the negative energy with feelings of frustration and self-criticism: "What's wrong with me? Why can't I do this?"

Like meditation and mindfulness practices, pratipaksha bhavana is best served by an easy-does-it approach. Replacement thoughts, whether verbal or visual, can be softly added, gently introduced, tenderly coaxed. Let your mantra be "Less strain, more gain."

We are well-advised to let the turbulent energy dissipate before attempting the replacement. Take a few minutes to do a calm-inducing breathing practice. Meditate. Listen to calming music. If appropriate, get away from your current setting and reboot. "It is very difficult to control negative thoughts while staying in a negative environment unless we have extraordinary strength," says Swami Satchidananda. "The easiest way is to change the environment." Go for a walk. Take a swim. Play with kids. Whatever it takes to lower the negative energy and lift the mood. This alone will be useful if Paul Brunton is correct that "The extent of the karmic consequences of an act will be proportionate to the energy it holds."

Alternatively, sit down, close your eyes, and shift your attention from the head to the rest of your body. Because thoughts have physical correlates, mental turbulence will be reflected in bodily sensations, and your attention will be drawn to the most intense ones. If you allow yourself simply to feel what's going on, making no effort to curtail or alter the sensations, the turmoil will eventually subside and your mind will follow suit. At some point, and it won't be long even if it feels interminable, the managerial part of your mind will find it easier to do the equivalent of sending in a relief pitcher, even if the starting pitcher is reluctant to leave the mound.

Patience pays. Remember the kshanti paramita? It means patience, and it's wise to apply it in the context of pratipaksha bhavana. Best to do what Ralph Waldo Emerson suggested: "Adopt the pace of nature: her secret is patience."

It takes time to cultivate new skills. Our minds have acquired habitual ways of reacting to events, and those patterns are linked to the residue of past impressions—not just wounds and traumas, mind you, but also pleasures and joys and happy experiences. In the yoga tradition, these deep impressions are known as *samskaras* and *vasanas,* and the more deeply embedded they are the longer it takes to dislodge them or to replace them with templates that produce positive thoughts, effective actions, and beneficial karma. Therefore, don't be shocked when the toxic thoughts you want to evict don't just politely leave. And be kind to yourself. You haven't failed. With patient persistence the ability to spot negative thoughts as they arise will take hold and you'll find it easier and easier to insert a benign replacement. Many practitioners eventually find that they're barely conscious of the process, just as we drive without thinking about each movement of the steering wheel.

The Best of Intentions

I know someone who has always aspired to be wealthy. He's achieved considerable success over the years, but has not yet reached the heights he envisions. He asked me if it's bad karma that the desire for money occupies so much of his thinking and is a prime organizing principle for his day-to-day life.

I gave him the only possible answer: "It depends."

Depends on what? Here's a partial list: How does he plan to acquire the wealth he dreams of? Will he earn it in a manner that benefits society, or in a way that damages the environment, the social fabric, or the health of consumers? Is he compromising his integrity to get what he's after? Does he work toward his goal honestly and ethically, or is he willing to deceive, exploit, and mistreat others on the way up? How much wealth would satisfy him, or would he always crave more? Why does he want to be rich in the first place? To boost his ego? To prove his worth? To get revenge on the jerks who teased him in high school? Or to provide a good life for his loved ones, give back to his community, or fund a philanthropy that cures disease or helps solve intractable social problems? Does he care at all about any of these issues?

In other words, what's going on in his mind?

"People often assume karma is only about external action," writes Sadhguru Jaggi Vasudev. "They think performing acts of charity and virtue will earn them good karma. What they never quite realize is that it is about something much subtler."[55] That subtle something is what the Indic traditions call *sankalpa* (sometimes spelled *samkalpa*). It means intention, or as some prefer, motivation, resolve, or volition. It's a subtle orientation that gives shape and direction to every thought, word, and deed, steering us like a rudder steers a ship. It's so instrumental that Buddha named *samma sankalpa* (right intent, or right resolve) one of the eight elements of his Noble Eightfold Path. Indeed, if the sages are correct, our intentions have a stronger impact on our karma than what we actually say and do.

This is analogous to what science has revealed about the layering of the material world: the deeper levels—in physics, subatomic particles; in human life, thought, feeling, intention, awareness—have greater potential power than the gross levels. It also holds up to common sense when we consider how individuals respond to different situations and how society constructs and implements its laws. Actions that are planned—premeditated as would be said in court—carry more weight than the same actions performed inadvertently, mistakenly, or reflexively. We treat a child who accidentally hurts a sibling different from one who deliberately inflicts pain. We even say "It's the thought that counts" when someone gives us an unsuitable gift.

Buddhists cite three principal qualities that constitute "right intention": 1) renunciation of things transient or ephemeral, aka, the absence of attachment, 2) benevolence, aka the absence of ill will toward others, 3) non-harming, aka resolving not to cause harm to other beings (in other words, ahimsa). The epitome of right intent, therefore, would be to make our way in the world firmly resolved to bring happiness, peace, love, and all things good to everyone we encounter, with no desire to be rewarded or recognized for the effort. A tall order perhaps, and we'll surely come up short much of the time, but just holding the aspiration deep inside can elevate our minds and nudge our tongues and our bodies in the right direction.

Much like an organization's mission statement or the vows made by members of a group, sankalpa adds clarity to our commitments, direction to our will, and strength to our determination. It resets our moral GPS, keeping us steady on the high road. In a spiritual sense, it helps to sanctify our actions. That's why, before a meditation session, many Buddhists state their intention for the practice to enhance the peace and happiness of all beings. And many Hindu rituals are preceded by a sankalpa that states the benevolent purpose of what is about to take place.

If every word we utter and every action we take, however automatic and spontaneous they might seem, is rooted in some form of sankalpa, wouldn't it make sense to become more conscious of our deepest intentions? Wouldn't it be wise to be more deliberate about the tone and tenor of the thoughts that motivate us? To nurture what we plant in the soil of our minds with the same care we give to the seeds we embed in our gardens? To be, so to speak, intentional about our intentions?

The logical first step would be to pay attention to the subtle impulses that move us to speak and act in particular ways. "In each of us, there are wholesome and unwholesome roots—or seeds—in the depths of our consciousness," Thich Nhat Hanh explains. "The practice of mindfulness helps us identify all the seeds in our store of consciousness and water the ones that are the most wholesome."[56]

In other words, we can peek beneath the surface of our thoughts and locate our intent before we initiate an action. We can discern whether we're coming from love and kindness or from greed, envy, or some other unsavory motive. Then, when necessary, we can course-correct by tabling a karmically detrimental intent in favor of a nobler one.

We can also be mindful after the fact. Did something go awry? Did I upset someone? Did I say or do something that is likely to reap unwanted consequences? If we can identify our underlying intentions and ask ourselves how we might elevate them in the future, we are already modifying our karma.

In the case of more deliberate actions, when we have the time to contemplate and plan—beginning a new venture, for example—why not think through exactly why we want to do what we're about to do? What do we really intend to happen? Once we're clear about our expected outcome, a good next step might be to raise the bar a bit and contemplate not only what's in it for us but how our actions might benefit others. Once formulated, the sankalpa can be articulated in a suitable manner: voiced quietly, perhaps, or silently as something like a prayer. Or put into writing, like a diary entry or a memo to oneself. Expressing it in a concrete way can help imprint the sankalpa in the depths of awareness.

Some teachers recommend formulating and expressing a sankalpa for the coming day first thing in the morning. Think of it as a vow, a resolution, or an affirmation. It could be a straightforward declarative statement along the lines of, "I intend this day to ___." If you're an adherent of a religious tradition, it might take the shape of a formal prayer or a sacred pledge, as in, "Lord, I promise that today I will ___." Buddhists favor statements beginning with "May," e.g., "May I treat everyone I encounter this day with lovingkindness." It should go without saying that karmic law does not stand on ceremony; the formal structure of a sankalpa amounts to little compared to the sincerity with which it is expressed—not what's on the page or the lips, but what's in the heart.

Taking stock at the end of the day by evaluating the degree to which we lived up to our sankalpa is also recommended. Paramahansa Yogananda suggested something like that as a bedtime routine, advising devotees to introspect honestly, take stock of any ways in which they fell short, and write down how they intend to do better the next day. Such practices can chart the way to improved karma and also serve as measuring rods with which to gauge our progress.

Formulating an overarching sankalpa for our lives can also be a powerful practice, providing a strong wind of moral intention for navigating the realm of karma. You might want to think about how to describe your most virtuous aspirations and the motives you would like to drive your actions. Consider putting it in writing, even if you're the only one who will read it. The clearer and more specific you can be, the better.

Two Karmic Superpowers

In his memoir, *Tales of Wonder,* scholar of religion Huston Smith wrote about the grueling month he'd once spent in Japan at a Zen monastery. When the retreat concluded, the master made some enigmatic remarks that left Smith confused about what Zen actually is. When pressed, the teacher summed things up with a simple instruction: "Make your whole life unceasing gratitude."

Similar things have been said about another virtue, compassion. The Dalai Lama for example: "Only the development of compassion and understanding for others can bring us the tranquility and happiness we all seek."

Gratitude and compassion are all-purpose thought replacers, karmic assets that have been extolled and encouraged by every spiritual tradition in history and now have the added distinction of a growing body of scientific evidence that confirms their benefits. They also have another distinct advantage: they can be refined, developed, and cultivated.

Gratitude: attitude, not platitude

There is so much empirical evidence that grateful thinking enhances measures of well-being—decreased depression and anxiety; greater resilience and disease resistance; less anger, resentment, and envy; more happiness; stronger relationships, etc.—that therapists and physicians often prescribe formal gratitude practices. Shifting the mind to a grateful gear is relatively easy to do, since we can always find things in our lives for which to be thankful. Many of those we typically take for granted: the roof over our heads, the hot running water, the food in the fridge, the books on our shelves, the friendly neighbors, the love of our families.

Gratitude can be invoked any time we think of it. Making it a regular practice, however, ensures that we remember. The most commonly prescribed process is to set aside time, every night or morning, once a week, or whatever frequency suits you best, to write down one thing you're grateful for—or two, or three, or more. To spice up the challenge, consider adding this proviso: include in each session something you've never listed before. One advantage to making the practice a routine is that it keeps us on the lookout for little godsends, making it much more likely that we feel grateful more of the time.

Keep in mind one of the notable discoveries researchers have made: gratitude can't be easily faked. Going through the motions, they found, is relatively useless. To reap the rewards, you actually have to feel grateful. But authentic gratitude is never very far away; if we pay attention and open our hearts, we can train ourselves to spot blessings the way bird watchers learn to detect feathered friends.

Passion for compassion

This staple of spiritual virtues has also earned scientific validation. Research at institutions like Stanford's Center for Compassion and Altruism Research and Education has yielded an impressive body of data on compassion's impact on the body, the brain, and outward behavior. In short, it's good for both the person who receives compassion and for the one who gives it, or even thinks it.

In addition to improvements on standard well-being metrics, compassion enhances human interaction and strengthens social bonds. It's even good for the bottom line, in case you think it will make you too soft to get ahead in the dog-eat-dog world. Turns out that business dogs respond better to kindness than to bared teeth. An online article in *Harvard Business Review*[57] cited studies that support the notion that compassion pays dividends. In one, a fourteen-year longitudinal study by the University of California, Berkeley's Haas School of Business, "selfish, aggressive, and manipulative" employees were less likely to climb the ladder than their "generous and agreeable" counterparts. A study from the University of South Carolina showed that Americans and Europeans with "prosocial motivation" earn more money than the self-interested. Another intriguing study tested nearly 3,000 Canadian kindergarten students. Following up *thirty years later*, researchers found that the now-grown lads who'd been kind to others had significantly higher incomes than those who'd been "aggressive or oppositional."

Call it career karma. But before you turn on the charm at work, here's a familiar caveat from the authors of the Harvard article: "Research also shows that motives do matter. If you display kindness or compassion to others for strategic or selfish reasons, you might as well forget it. Research shows that you have to be authentically altruistic—not strategically helping others or forced into it—or it won't work."

Fortunately, compassion can be cultivated. Scientists at academic institutions such as Emory and Stanford have studied the neuro-correlates of compassion and have developed training programs using both eastern and western methods. Buddhists long ago developed practices to draw compassion and loving-kindness out from the recesses of our hearts and make their expression more natural and spontaneous. Two traditional methods, *Metta* and *Tonglen* have become widely employed in the West, and not just among those who identify as Buddhists.

Metta. You'll find numerous variations of Metta (typically translated as "lovingkindness"), all of which follow the same basic pattern: inwardly evoke compassion for oneself, then extend the feeling outward to others further and further from our normal range of concern. Here is one variation.

Sit in a quiet, comfortable place, as you would for any form of meditation or mindfulness. When you feel relaxed, recite the following sentences inwardly, pausing a moment between each. Take note of any feelings or sensations that arise.

May I be free from suffering.

May I be healthy and strong.

May I be peaceful and at ease.

May I be happy.

Rest for a minute or two, or longer if you would like. Then shift the focal point of attention from yourself to someone you care about, replacing "I" with the person's name:

May [name] be free from suffering.

May [name] be healthy and strong.

May [name] be peaceful and at ease.

May [name] be happy.

Rest for a short period of time and take note of how different or similar the experience was from when you directed compassion to yourself.

Now switch to someone for whom you have neutral feelings, perhaps an acquaintance, a co-worker, or a distant relative. Recite the same phrases inwardly, only with the new person's name. Again, rest and take note of how it felt compared to the previous series.

Continue as before, only this time focus on someone for whom you have unfriendly feelings—someone who annoys you, perhaps, or for whom you harbor animosity, or with whom you have some kind of conflict. Insert that person's name in the sentences you intone inwardly.

This time around you might feel resistance; carry on as sincerely as you can. During the rest phase, reflect on the thoughts and feelings that came up, and ponder what might need to happen for you to express compassion for that person and really mean it.

In the final phase, shift your attention to the welfare of everyone on the planet. Begin each sentence with "May all beings . . ." Again, note whether the experience is different. Most people find it pleasant and heartwarming to wish the best for all of humanity.

Tonglen. Another Buddhist practice, Tonglen (Tibetan for "giving and taking" or "sending and receiving") is a different way of directing compassion outward to alleviate suffering. It can be done as a formal sitting practice and/or at any time one feels moved to do it. Here is the sitting version, which can easily be adapted for other uses.

Sit in a comfortable, meditative position with eyes closed. Think of someone who is suffering in some way, whether from physical pain, mental turmoil, emotional anguish, or otherwise. It could be someone you care deeply about or a peripheral acquaintance or even someone you've never met. Imagine the person standing before you, enveloped by a visual representation of suffering—a dark cloud, for example, or noxious fumes.

Breathe in deeply, imagining that you are pulling the toxic shroud away from the person and drawing it into your own chest. Imagine it becoming lighter and purer inside of you, turning into a radiant light made of lovingkindness. Allow the light to fill you up.

As you exhale, project that resplendent light outward from your heart to embrace the suffering person and alleviate their burdens. Continue in this manner for a while, inhaling the shroud of suffering and exhaling the radiant glow of compassion.

Buddhist teachers suggest that once you're used to doing tonglen as a sitting practice, you can use it at other times as well. For example, when you're on a bus or train and see someone who appears to be upset; when you see images of warfare or disaster in the news; when you visit a friend who's ill; in the midst of an argument. Just visualize the dark energy; breathe it into yourself; transform it into light; and breathe out radiant compassion.

People sometimes ask whether Metta and Tonglen actually affect the individuals the practitioner intends to help. I don't know if that can be answered, but experience clearly indicates that practitioners themselves benefit. The practices are calming and elevating in the moment, and their regular use enhances one's capacity for compassion just as lifting weights strengthens one's muscles. "If we cultivate lovingkindness," write Joseph Goldstein and Jack Kornfield in *Seeking the Heart of Wisdom*, "we experience its taste in the moment and at the same time are strengthening it as a force in the mind, making it easier for it to arise again."

When you think about it, what would pave the way to better karma more than making compassion, or loving-kindness, the foundational mindset for every sentence we utter and every action we take?

Additional Thoughts on Thought

Attending to the mental patterns that underpin our actions is like correcting physiological imbalances that make us susceptible to disease. Our task is to lift our intentions, perceptions, attitudes, and desires out of the shadows of the unconscious, where they tend to reside, and into the forefront of awareness. We can detect them as they arise, let the karmically wholesome ones pass through, and nudge aside the less virtuous ones to make room for an upgrade. By consciously and consistently elevating the contents of our minds, we can, over time, change our default settings, because every thought—like every action we take—leaves an impression, and the patterns those impressions form become the behavioral tendencies that shape our character.

Bear in mind that making such changes is far from automatic.

Nor is it guaranteed that our behavior will always comply with our conscious intentions, however sincere we may be. Our egos will sometimes betray our aspirations. Noble motives will sometimes get elbowed aside by selfish ones. Our bad habits won't get dislodged all at once. Our systems won't instantly be purged of all the old impressions that condition our behavior. Transformation requires effort, persistence, and patience.

That said, the main takeaway is that the mix of energies that determine our karma include not only the spirit behind the actions we take but also the thoughts and feelings we *don't* act upon. Suppose, for example, you're obsessed with getting even with someone and ceaselessly fantasize about beating him up, but never go the next step. Can it be said that, because you never laid a hand on the guy, you're practicing ahimsa? On the surface, yes, you're certainly closer to the spirit of ahimsa than if you were to actually commit assault. But the karma attached to violence will nevertheless accrue to some degree, depending on the intensity and duration of your pugnacious thoughts. Similarly, you might be all smiles while doing something charitable, like volunteering at a soup kitchen, but if you're seething with resentment because you're not being thanked enough, well, the karmic boost won't be quite as high as it would be if you were to perform your service with a selfless, loving heart.

The same principle applies to the positive side of the ledger. If we have kind, compassionate thoughts about someone, we accrue beneficial karma even if we're unable to act on those feelings or give voice to them. In the same way, holding the sincere intent to be a better human being is, by itself, karmically advantageous. The more we remind ourselves of our noblest sankalpa the more engrained it becomes, and the more likely our speech and actions will follow suit. The repetition is like making small deposits to a bank account; the karma adds up with interest. (Conversely, it is said that each time a negative behavior is repeated, it accrues more karmic debt than it did the previous time.) Buddhists, for example, aspire to *dana,* which means the act of giving. But they recognize that we can give for selfish reasons, like wanting to be celebrated as a generous person or to be owed something in return. Therefore, they attempt to cultivate *caga,* a state of mind that's naturally oriented to generosity. For those with true caga, the act of giving is said to be effortless. Moreover, having caga and failing to act generously is better karmically than giving things away *without* caga. It's kind of like doing poorly on an exam but getting an A for effort. Or, as my mother used to tell me when I whined about another kid screwing up, "He means well, honey."

To add further nuance, consider that every action we take not only generates reciprocal karma; it also conditions the mind going forward by strengthening either positive or negative tendencies.

Also factoring into the karmic calculus is our state of mind *after* taking action. As Radhakrishnan puts it in *Indian Philosophy*, "Karma is an act both intellectual and volitional. . . . Psychologically every act has three sides: (1) volitional preparation, (2) the act itself, and (3) what is called the 'back' of the act." By back he means the thoughts and feelings that follow the action. Do you become arrogant or self-righteous because you did something good? That produces different karma than being humble and self-effacing. Feeling regret when you hurt someone is obviously different from having schadenfreude, that wonderful German term for deriving pleasure from the misfortune of others. We know this instinctively; that's why criminal courts are more lenient with defendants who express remorse.

The back of the act concept is nicely illustrated by this teaching story related by the aforementioned authors, Goldstein and Kornfield. A man offers food to a passing monk, a custom that was held to produce very good karma. Afterward, the man regrets what he'd done, thinking he'd wasted good food on an ascetic. What was the karmic result? Because he made the offering, it is said, the man was born into wealth for seven straight incarnations.

But his regret was costly; he was destined to spend each of those lives as an unhappy miser.

Finally, a cautionary note. Some of the thought patterns that create negative karma can be modified with attention and will power, as we've discussed in this chapter. Others are amenable to elimination or amelioration through yogic methodologies and spiritual practices, as we'll see in the next chapter. But others might be the result of factors such as compulsion, obsession, or addiction, which are beyond the scope of this book. Professional help might be called for.

In my many years on the path, speaking to spiritual aspirants both casually and in interviews, I've seen a certain amount of resistance to seeking psychotherapeutic help. The assumption (or dream) that all our psychological and emotional baggage can be eliminated through spiritual practice—or will come to be seen as illusory or piddling in the glow of divine light—has proved to be erroneous. Persisting in that belief at the expense of our relationships, careers, and physical and mental health has properly been labeled "spiritual bypassing." Steering clear of psychotherapy may have made sense fifty years ago, when the great majority of professionals had no sympathy for, or understanding of, spirituality or contemplative practices. Back then, people were known to dash to therapists and physicians when what they were going through was not a sign of pathology but a genuine and valuable spiritual emergence. Sadly, many were incorrectly diagnosed and needlessly medicated. But it should also be noted that some seekers have insisted on viewing their psychological tumult as a sign of spiritual breakthrough, only to regret not finding help.

Circumstances are different now. It's no longer difficult to find a therapist who's not only properly credentialed but spiritually fluent. In fact, one of the more interesting developments in contemporary spirituality is the integration of modern depth psychology and ancient wisdom. Notable influencers have brought

Carl Jung's insights about the so-called shadow elements of the psyche into the realm where therapy meets spiritual unfoldment. "No matter the spiritual path we choose, we inevitably encounter our own shadow," writes psychologist Connie Zweig in *Meeting the Shadow on the Spiritual Path.* Recognizing, understanding, and working effectively with those buried elements can be an integral aspect of mature spiritual development, and certainly a sound karmic investment.

If you find yourself in need of professional help, ask your friends, colleagues, and spiritual companions for referrals. Find out if any members of your spiritual community are mental health experts. Check the bulletin boards of yoga studios, meditation centers, houses of worship, and natural food stores. See if your healthcare provider or local mental health clinic can refer you to the right person. Search online for the referral services of professional organizations such as the American Psychological Association and the Association for Transpersonal Psychology. And once you get the ball rolling, don't necessarily settle for one opinion; get a second, and maybe a third and a fourth if necessary.

Karmic patterns are like stains: some can be rubbed out; some are as obstinate as red wine. For the latter, we can use all the help we can get.

7

Practice Makes Less Imperfect

"You're bound to become a Buddha if you practice. If water drips long enough even rocks wear through."—*Shih-wu*

When she was a month shy of her forty-eighth birthday, my mother swallowed a vial of sleeping pills and lay down to die. I was the only other person in the house at the time. When I realized that she wasn't just napping, I froze in indecision like Arjuna in the Bhagavad Gita. Do I call for an ambulance? Try to shake her awake? Let her go? My vacillation lasted only a moment; it seemed crystal clear that, in that instance, right action meant *no* action.

I don't know if I'd ever heard the word karma at the time, but if I had I would not have given it much thought. I just knew my mother had terminal cancer and was determined to spare herself and those she loved unnecessary suffering. By doing nothing I was doing what she would have wanted.

In the decades since, I've never once regretted my decision, or even questioned it. When working on this book, however, I reflected on that pivotal moment and wondered about the karmic implications. Every religious tradition I'm aware of frowns upon suicide. The details vary, but in general taking one's own life is considered a sin in the West and bad karma in the East. So, I pondered: What karma did my mother acquire for taking the step she chose to take? What karmic consequences followed from my choice not to intervene? What was my father's karma for panicking when he came home and rushing his beloved to a hospital for futile rescue efforts?

Clearly, everyone's motivation was grounded in love, and no one intended to cause harm. All good, right? Surely, we're off the hook, karmically speaking.

And yet I can't help but wonder if there are karmic nuances that elude me. How would our karma have changed if we'd made different decisions? Looking at the bigger picture, how does karma explain why my mother, a kind and decent human being, was destined to suffer and die at a young age? What karmic lessons was my father meant to learn from his loss? Ditto for my brother and me? And what were the karmic threads that knit our souls into a family quilt in the first place? I think as well about the choices others would have made in the same circumstances: a Catholic who believes that suicide is a mortal sin; a physician who has sworn to save lives under any circumstances; a lawyer or police officer in a location where abetting suicide is a criminal offense. Would their karma have been calculated differently?

In the end, we return to the same astute insight: the details of karma are ultimately unknowable. When we're caught up in a complex human drama, we can only speculate about the karmic causes that led to that moment and the potential karmic effects of what we elect to do or not do. In my case, if any conscious reasoning transpired at the moment of decision, it would have been too swift and too hazy to register. For all intents and purposes I acted intuitively, but with no less conviction than if I'd asked an AI app to sort through all the world's knowledge and arrive at a rational choice.

So, we return to the core question: How, in any given situation, can we know which words and actions will maximize good karma and minimize bad? Sometimes it's as clear as spring water—a choice between helping and harming, or between telling the truth and lying—but at other times it's as murky as mud. The laws of karma are not encoded in well-indexed and cross-referenced volumes like municipal lawbooks. We can turn to moral codes and behavioral precepts, but as we've seen, they too have to be interpreted and adapted to specific, sometimes unprecedented circumstances. We can analyze all the variables based on what we know, but complexity tends to increase uncertainty, so we're often reduced to contemplating the unknown. We can go with our guts, but while our intuition might sometimes seem impeccable, it's often sabotaged by our own rattled minds and usurped by intruders like fear, denial, and wishful thinking. And even if we discern the most karmically auspicious option, there's no guarantee we'll act accordingly, because, after all, the demon on one shoulder can be more persuasive than the angel on the other. As Paul said in the New Testament, speaking for all of us at times, "What I want to do I do not do, but what I hate I do."

By way of a remedy for this karmic imprecision, the Eastern traditions proposed a strategy more efficacious than either reason alone or simply muddling through. They developed methods to align mind, body, and spirit with the intelligence that runs the cosmos, thereby increasing the likelihood that we'll think virtuous thoughts, feel life-enhancing emotions, make benevolent choices, and take the most karmically advantageous actions.

The Good Karma Two-Step

I first read the Bhagavad Gita in my early days on the spiritual path. To me, it was a sacred text, a philosophical treatise, a self-help manual, and a non-sectarian guide to living all wrapped up in one. It's been a lodestar ever since, and one sentence above all has lit my way: "Established in Yoga, perform action" (chapter 2, verse 48). I can neither read nor write Sanskrit, but from the first time I heard the phrase in that language I've never forgotten it: *Yogastah kuru karmani*. As a taut synopsis of Yoga philosophy, nothing I'm aware of rivals those few words. Nor can I think of a more practical formula for living well and doing good on the spinning wheel of karma.

"Established in Yoga" does not mean mastering a set of stretches and bends to YouTube-worthy perfection. It refers to the larger meaning of Yoga as expressed, notably, at the beginning of the Yoga Sutras (1, 2): "Yoga is the cessation of the fluctuations of mind-stuff" (in Sanskrit, *Yogash chitta vritti nirodhah*).[58] The definition points to a quieting of the infamous Monkey Mind, and ultimately to silent awareness without thought, aka consciousness alone in its pure, primordial state. In the aphorism that follows (1, 3), Patanjali explains that when that transcendence of thought occurs, "Then the seer is revealed, abiding in its own essential nature, and one realizes the true Self."

That might sound abstract, but in reality it's quite simple—the simplest state imaginable in fact—and in practical terms the implications are profound. Stilling the incessant chatter in our heads is as natural as enabling a pot of boiling water to settle into a calm equilibrium by turning off the flame. Exactly *how* to do that is the obvious question, and we'll get to it soon. But first, let's take full note that Yoga is herein defined as a state of being, not as an activity one does or an exercise one performs. That's why I'm spelling it with a capital Y, in contrast to yoga *practice*, which gets the small y treatment. In other words, the aim of doing yoga is to achieve Yoga.

One characteristic of that state is captured in the typical translation of "yoga" as union. It means that the individual self and the universal Self—the essential nature of all that is—are unified (and, in reality, were never *not* One). And, to repeat Patanjali, in that state of unification "one realizes the true Self."[59] The traditional use of the upper case in Self is to emphasize that our deepest nature is contiguous with the ultimate reality that underlies and permeates all of existence. It is beyond the egoic, embodied personality with which we usually identify, and is also *beyond the range of karma*. No karma can be produced in the transcendent, where there are no boundaries, no separate entities, no causes, no effects—only Oneness. The Self is absolute, eternal, and infinite. And, as the famous maxim in the Upanishads informs us, *Thou art That*.

We are all That. And it is said that those who truly and enduringly awaken to that fundamental truth—those who are permanently "established in Yoga"—exist in a state of supreme fulfillment, peace, and bliss. They are also said to be liberated from the bondage of karma and free of the conditioning effects of past impressions. From the penthouse view of human development as described by the Eastern sages, the kind of karma we think of as good is actually as binding as the opposite kind. Both are shackles, it is said, only one is made of gold and the other of iron. The twentieth-century sage Ramana Maharshi put it this way: "The deeds we do in a dream do not touch our 'waking' life and slip away when we 'awake.' Our deeds done in this clouded ego life disappear and leave no trace when we wake up, in the divine white light of Self-Awareness."

How can that be possible when even the most fully enlightened human beings still retain personalities and inhabit bodies that walk around doing things in the realm where karmic law prevails? The answer to that question is too complex and subtle to rummage around in here. Suffice it to say that what shifts for the awakened individual is what we might call the center of gravity or the fulcrum of orientation. The body and mind continue to create and experience karma, but no one is home so to speak. One's address has relocated from the embodied ego, i.e., the finite self, to the infinite Self, and, as Paramahansa Yogananda wrote in his autobiography, "The iron filings of karma are attracted only where a magnet of the personal ego still exists."

The enlightened ones that Hindus call *jivanmuktis* and

Buddhists call *arhats* are said to be sublimely content, exhibiting what the Bhagavad Gita refers to as "equanimity in gain and loss, pleasure and pain, victory and defeat." They dwell in divine light, where the play of karma is just so many passing shadows. "Just as in bright sunlight candlelight loses its relative significance," wrote Maharishi Mahesh Yogi, "so also in the eternal light of absolute bliss do the relative joys of life lose their fast grip on the mind. Thus, the mind is freed from the binding influence of karma."[60] To top it off, those illumined souls do not have to endure another human existence; they have graduated from the School of Earth, summa cum laude.

At least that's what is said to be the case in sacred texts and thousands of discourses. One day, perhaps, science will develop the means to verify or disprove the proposition. What matters here are two things: 1) the possibility of such a lofty attainment seems more and more reasonable as one moves along the spiritual path and starts to see signposts that fit the description, and 2) the model has value for us semi-enlightened souls as we wrestle with karma like the biblical Jacob wrestled an angel.

The View from the Road

Whether we call it enlightenment, awakening, *moksha, nirvana,* or any of its other designations, to the extent that the permanently awakened state is attainable, it is undeniably rare. For the vast majority of spiritual seekers it's a long-term, perhaps multi-incarnational, prospect. As an aspiration it should not be discounted, and no consideration of karma can ignore what has been said about it. As a practical matter, though, what commands our attention is the transformative progress that occurs en route. In that regard, awakening is an ideal to hold before us and to learn from, just as an aspiring artist views masterworks in a museum.

Suppose you've spent your entire life in a desert. One day

you hear about something called an ocean, where there are cool breezes, moist air, and a large body of water—all, perhaps, things you can only imagine. You set out in the direction to which you were pointed, determined to reach this paradise if it really exists. At some point along the way, you start to hear a sound you've never heard before: waves crashing on a sandy beach. Soon you begin to feel cooler. You sense something salty in the air. You feel moisture on your skin. You come upon groves of palm trees. Underfoot, the soil changes texture. And one day you see in the distance an expanse of blue. All of these clues tell you that the ocean you'd heard about might actually be out there. You step up your pace with eager confidence. And you start to realize that if the ocean turns out not to be as advertised, or if you never get to dip your toe into it, you'll still be glad you took the journey because you've experienced life in a whole new beautiful way.

Spiritual progress is like that. If we march along the path with diligence, discernment, and dignity, we experience along the way tastes of nirvana, sips of moksha, glimpses of infinity. Not only is this satisfying in and of itself, it also gives us incentive to keep on trucking, and in the process our lives are transformed. Spiritual progress is marked by the presence, however fleeting, of qualities said to characterize enlightenment: inner peace, joy, contentment, bliss; acute perception, expanded awareness, a magnified sense of identity; clear, quiet mind; greater capacity for compassion, kindness, and love. Such attributes are not only confirmation that we're headed in the right direction, they're also the keys to a transformed relationship with karma.

In other words, the first step of "Established in Yoga, perform action" is to turn inward toward the silent, unified state of being at our core. Step two is to return to the outer world having been purified and cleansed to some degree, and better equipped to think, feel, speak, and act in a karmically beneficial way. The dynamic is not unlike Jesus's admonition to "seek ye first the kingdom of God" if you want to have good things added unto you. Or, if you prefer non-religious analogies, it's not unlike withdrawing cash from the ATM before heading to the farmer's market or stretching before taking off on a jog.

Fortunately, the wise ones of old did not just philosophize. As pragmatists, they developed methodologies for turning revelation into reality.

Sadhana

You've probably heard the old joke. A tourist in New York asks a pedestrian, "How do you get to Carnegie Hall?"

The answer: "Practice, practice, practice."

It's not just a punchline, and not just good advice for someone trying to master a skill. It's an essential nudge to those who want to reconfigure their karmic future. Practice is what makes the abstract concrete and the potential actual. It's what makes "Established in Yoga, perform action" an empirical, testable formula, not a religious precept or speculative philosophy. The practices developed by the Eastern explorers, who turned within instead of sailing the seas or peering through microscopes, modify the human apparatus in karmically advantageous ways, such as: cleansing the system of embedded impressions that condition perception and behavior; increasing inner stability and mental clarity; augmenting resilience in the face of change; fostering inner peace and contentment. As a result, the disciplines increase the likelihood that the practitioner will behave virtuously. They are also said to instill qualities that science can't yet measure, such as aligning the mind with the evolutionary intelligence that drives the cosmos, or, in spiritual terms, divine will. That last feature might sound esoteric, but for those who've tasted it in their lives it seems as practical as filling a prescription but with fewer side effects. As Joseph Campbell put it, "The goal of life is to make your heartbeat match the beat of the universe, to match your nature with Nature." Where karma is concerned, it doesn't get any better than that.

Based on my research, my personal experience, and the hundreds of interviews I've conducted, the most effective approach is to acquire a practice, or a coherent set of practices, and engage in it consistently. The yogic word for such a routine is *sadhana,* which has been translated as "go straight to a goal," "means to completion or perfection," and "method adopted to accomplish a specific goal." In everyday use, "regular practice" usually suffices.

It should be noted that establishing a routine does not mean never changing it. If a sadhana has any power, it will be transformative. As a result, the practitioner will change, and over time his or her needs will change, making it advisable to evaluate one's routine periodically and to modify it accordingly. We should also note that one's sadhana might consist of a combination of methods that can done sequentially but also separately. One more note: it is highly efficacious to supplement one's regular sadhana with a repertoire of additional practices to be undertaken as needed at other times in one's life. (We'll come back to that later in the chapter.)

Eight intersecting limbs

In the yogic tradition, the standard pattern of a multifaceted sadhana is to move from the gross to the subtle to the transcendent, more or less addressing the five koshas, or layers of selfhood, in order (see chapter 6). The classic eight limbs of Yoga sequentially take the attention from outer behavior to physical activity to deeper and deeper internalization. As we've seen, limbs one and two, *yama* and *niyama,* consist of behavioral guidelines, i.e., what to abstain from and what to nurture. The rest are:

Limb 3, asana. The word *asana*, meaning posture, position, or pose, is now associated with the stretches and bends we see in yoga studios, magazines, and videos. In fact, those exercises make no appearance in the Yoga Sutras, where asana is mentioned only with regard to the ideal sitting posture for meditation. The familiar asana postures, which derive from the Hatha Yoga tradition, typically take the lead in a sadhana routine. The value of a good sequence of postures for ironing out tension, clearing out some of the physical residue of past experiences, and preparing the body and mind for subsequent practices is well accepted.

Limb 4, pranayama. Literally meaning control of the vital life force (*prana*), pranayama is mainly associated with breath control and formal breathing exercises. When performed properly, pranayama energizes subtle aspects of the physiology and cleanses the pranamaya kosha. As a result, blockages are eliminated, breath becomes easier to regulate, and prana flows to where it is needed. Hundreds of pranayama variations have been developed and refined by yogis over the centuries, some easy and gentle and others forceful and more challenging to master. But even simple breathing practices have the immediate effect of deepening repose.

Limb 5, pratyahara. Search the term *pratyahara* and you'll find two translations: sense control and withdrawal of the senses from their objects. While traditional teachings include in this category methods for mastering the senses and shrinking their dominance, in the context of sadhana, pratyahara begins the process of redirecting attention from the outer to the inner. We all reduce distraction by closing our eyes or canceling noise by shutting the door so we can think more clearly. Similarly, we block out as much sensory stimulation as possible when going to sleep. Pratyahara might include steps like that, but it implies something far more profound: a turn toward transcending the senses and the mind entirely.

Limb 6, dharana. Here's where things start to get tricky. Dharana is usually translated as concentration or, "focusing the mind on a single object." That sounds simple enough, but in practice different interpretations have led to widely divergent disciplines. Some concentration practices instruct practitioners to fix their minds on an object—something internal like a body part or a visual object like a burning candle—and hold it there for an extended period of time. In that category, methods vary widely in the degree of control and intensity of effort they demand. Other interpretations of *dharana* see it not as a sustained act of concentration but a gentle turning of attention to an object—the breath, a visualized image, a mantra—as a kind of launching pad for the next limb.

Limb 7, dhyana. As noted in chapter four, dhyana is virtually always translated as meditation. The word derives from two Sanskrit roots, *dhi*, meaning "mind," and *yana*, "moving." That derivation has given rise to dhyana being described as the movement of the mind in a sustained direction—a reasonable image of what tends to occur in traditional meditation practice. One also runs across definitions that conflate dhyana and dharana (erroneously, I believe) by saying dhyana focuses the mind on an object. That implies mind control, whereas in most forms of dhyana practitioners are told to allow the fleeting objects of attention to come and go without judgement, attachment, or manipulation. The term "steadiness" that's often associated with dhyana does not mean steady as in fixed or rigid, but steady as in continuous. As Radhakrishnan puts it, "Dhyana is the steady endeavor to bring the mind into harmony with all that is."[61] In other words, dhyana is often distinguished by the *absence* of focus, a release of control that allows attention to sink like a diving bell to deeper, more silent levels of the mind.

There is much more to be said about meditation, and we'll get to that momentarily. For now, it should be noted that the four previous limbs are usually taken to be preparation for this one: asana relaxes the body; pranayama settles the breath; the senses are turned inward; a mental object is introduced; meditation commences. It's all in the service of that definition of Yoga we examined earlier: the cessation of the fluctuations of mind-stuff. Which brings us to the pure stillness of the final limb.

Limb 8, samadhi. This is not an activity or a practice; it's a state of being, in fact the very state of yogic unity we've discussed. *Samadhi* is given insufficient currency in modern yoga circles because it's seen as a long-term and rarely achievable goal. That's certainly true of the advanced states of samadhi, but in its most elementary form it often arises as a momentary event in a productive sadhana session, sometimes so fleeting and undramatic that practitioners don't know it's occurred until it's described to them.

The most frequent translation of samadhi is "absorption," sometimes expanded to "absorption in the object of attention (or meditation)." That attempt to clarify actually backfires because it gives the impression that samadhi is the same thing as one-pointed concentration on a mantra or an image. It's not, because in samadhi the perception of objects ceases. The mind itself is transcended. What gets absorbed is the small self into the big Self—in Buddhist terms, the apparent self into no-self. In other words, "absorption into the object of meditation" makes sense only if the "object" is ultimate Reality, which is not actually an object at all.

If this sounds confusing, blame it on the inadequacy of language to describe the ineffable. Try looking at it this way. Ordinary experience consists of an experiencer (the conscious individual), an object of experience (either an external or an internal one), and a process of experience that mediates between subject and object. In samadhi they all melt into one another. No object, only subject; no process of experience, only the experiencer alone in all its fullness. Which makes what we call the *experience* of samadhi a misnomer because it's not really an experience but more of an event or an occurrence. Think of it as awareness becoming aware of itself, or consciousness in isolation as opposed to the familiar experience of being conscious *of* something. It's Oneness. It's simply Being, where we mind our own Is-ness and there is no doing and therefore no karma.

It should be noted that the same phenomenon of transcendence is also called *turiya,* which means "fourth," in this case a fourth state of consciousness qualitatively different from the familiar three of waking, sleeping, and dreaming. In addition, as noted earlier, several types, or levels, of samadhi are described in the literature. Suffice it to say that the temporary glimpses of samadhi that might occur in meditation—or perhaps spontaneously from what we call grace—can develop over time into more sustained and even permanent states. That said, two forms should be noted because they are more commonly encountered than we realize: *nirvikalpa samadhi,* in which pure consciousness is revealed in the absence of objects; and *savikalpa samadhi,* in which that same unblemished awareness silently witnesses the thoughts and sensations that pass through the mind.

At this point, you might be asking, "Why are you weighing me down with these arcane explanations? I just want to manage my karma and make my life better."

My answer is: The teachings I'm drawing from are meant to be applied, and better understanding makes for better application, just as even rudimentary knowledge of how a smartphone app works makes its use less haphazard. Samadhi sounds abstract, but it's as practical as soap. By tapping into the Infinite, we essentially reach beyond the fog of karma to bring in the disinfectant of light. Referring to what he calls Presence, the spiritual teacher Eckhart Tolle says, "It is another dimension that breaks into the karmic realm. . . . [T]here's something totally from beyond karma, that can come into your life at any point."

What makes this immediately practical is that we emerge from such experiences cleansed and refreshed, as we would from a bath, better equipped to act in karmically beneficial ways.

The Wrong Impressions

Together, the eight limbs of Yoga constitute an ascending spiral of development, in that strengthening one limb strengthens the others. Hence, observing the yamas and niyamas makes the other practices more effective. In reverse, the effective use of those practices makes it easier and more natural to behave in accord with the yamas and niyamas, all to our karmic advantage. We not only have centuries of anecdotal evidence of this, but also abundant scientific research on the benefits of mindfulness, meditation, yoga asanas, and related practices.

It's common sense really. We all know that we're more prone to doing the wrong thing when we're frustrated, tense, aggravated, or worried, or when we feel put upon, victimized, or unfairly treated. Conversely, we're more likely to do the right thing when we feel happy, content, satisfied, appreciative, and calm. The Eastern traditions would put it this way: the nature and quality of our thoughts, motives, and intentions—and, as a consequence, our actions—are determined in large part by our underlying state of consciousness. Those states of consciousness are subject to change. As my earliest spiritual teacher, Maharishi Mahesh Yogi, was fond of saying, "Knowledge is different in different states of consciousness." It could also be said that *reality* is different in different states of consciousness, and thoughts are different, emotions are different, perception is different; so are reason, discernment, and intuition, as well as motivation, intention, and volition. Hence, the fundamental importance of practices that cultivate a quiet, clear, coherent state of consciousness.

Here's another way of looking at the karmic implications of sadhana. I mentioned earlier the cyclical pattern in which our actions in the world create impressions, which give rise to desires, which lead to actions, which create impressions, and on and on. In the yogic framework, the stored impressions are of two kinds: *samskaras* and *vasanas.* Sorting out the differences between the two gets a little arcane, and I've found a surprising lack of uniformity among experts. The prevailing view seems to be the following. Samskaras are impressions, or imprints, created by experience. They're like mental etchings whose grooves deepen with repetition and become character traits. Samskaras are often called "activators" because they trigger action. Vasanas (the term derives from the Sanskrit for "dwell") are essentially chains of samskaras that function like memories or latent tendencies to shape how we perceive the world. Apparently, the word also shares a root with the term for fragrance, causing some to compare vasanas to lingering scents, like cigarette smoke on clothing or, as Buddhist scholar Traleg Kyabgon put it, "smelly socks in a drawer."

For the sake of simplicity, let's fold samskara and vasana into the single term "impressions."

Those impressions are stored in what psychologists would call the subconscious and neuroscientists would call the central nervous system. Yogic thinkers divided that storehouse into the five koshas we discussed earlier. However we choose to envision the storage units, the embedded imprints are like planted seeds; they germinate into actions that are either karmically beneficial or karmically harmful. Some give rise only to a passing preference or an inconsequential decision; others, such as those reinforced through repetition, grow into habits, obsessions, compulsions, and even addictions. The stronger and more entrenched the impression, the more dominant it becomes, and the more likely it is to sprout into action—possibly a regrettable action.

Our task, then, is to weaken, neuter, or possibly eliminate the negative impressions, and to strengthen the positive ones. In addition, it's a good idea to conduct our lives in such a manner that the new impressions we create direct our behavior toward the higher realms of goodness. A transformative sadhana, supplemented by other psychospiritual practices and wise lifestyle choices, can play a major role in accomplishing those goals by reducing the binding influence of past impressions. Yogis refer to this as burning the seeds of karma in the fire of sadhana, because burnt seeds can't germinate.

Think of it this way: effective practices produce mental and physical stillness, and stillness heals. That's why animals curl up when injured, and why we're told to rest in bed when we get sick, and why we encase a broken bone to keep it from moving. Stillness restores integrity to wounded systems. Stillness promotes natural growth and evolution. The result is a form of purification not unlike cleansing the stale smoke from one's clothing, detoxing a body polluted by drugs, or kneading muscles to smooth out knots of tension.

Putting Practice into Practice

The most commonly recommended sequence for a sadhana based on classical Yoga is a set of asanas (yoga postures), followed by a period of pranayama (breathing exercises), and finally the inward turn leading to meditation and, possibly, a taste of samadhi. It's easy to see that this is a sequential flow from gross to subtle, or from the physical to the mental to the spiritual. It's not unlike a diver sinking from the turbulent surface of a lake to deeper strata where the current runs smoother, and finally to the utter stillness of the floor.

There are countless variations of that basic template. They differ regarding the specific practices prescribed (the diversity is huge), and also in the duration of each segment and the time span of a session as a whole. Traditionally, meditation is considered the key component and therefore given the most time. But these days, with the immense popularity of asana practice, that is not always the case. In any event, practitioners are advised to seek expert guidance in developing a routine that suits their individual needs, schedules, and lifestyles—subject to modification as circumstances change.

This is the point at which readers might understandably expect step-by-step instructions. I've chosen not to go there. I've learned from decades of experience that there are no one-size-fits-all formulas. Ideally, sadhana should be specifically tailored for each individual. In addition, the written word is clearly not the best way to transmit instructions. In the not-too-distant past, it might have made sense to put instructions in a book (I'm one of many who did so), but now, with so many opportunities for in-person learning—at yoga studios, meditation centers, fitness centers, churches and synagogues, healthcare facilities, etc.—and with online videos at our fingertips, why risk the mistakes that invariably come when trying to master a technique while reading instructions? Not to mention another obvious shortcoming of the printed page: it can't hear your questions.

Here are some tips to aid you in your search for effective practices. With respect to yoga asanas:

- Look for well-trained, certified teachers; give extra points to those who are affiliated with a reputable organization or a lineage that oversees teachers and offers students ongoing support.
- Tread lightly and carefully. Buddha called the body the "vehicle for awakening." Western traditions use the term "temple of the soul." It is all too easy to acquire an injury by stretching too far or bending in a way that's unsuitable for your physical condition. Find an experienced instructor who can give you some personal attention.
- Whether you have one yoga teacher or draw from many sources, assemble an easy-to-do asana sequence that suits your physiology and capabilities. Practicing at home on your own is different from doing it in a class under supervision, so keep it easy and safe.
- Consider having two or three routines at your disposal, to give you flexibility with respect to time and physical limitations.

- Favor a relaxing sequence. As a prelude to meditation, you want to let your engine slow to an even purr, not rev it up.
- Don't try to bend or stretch beyond your capacity, or strain to reach a difficult position.

With respect to breathing practices, some of the same advice pertains:

- Seek out qualified teachers.
- Learn a variety of pranayama methods to use according to your needs and circumstances. There are dozens, if not hundreds, ranging from easy, gentle, and natural to difficult, forceful, and rigorous.
- Play it safe and avoid strain. The chances of injury are less than with bending and stretching, but I once got so carried away with forceful exhales that I tore a muscle in my rib cage. And I've heard much worse stories.

Note that I've focused on methods from the Yoga tradition because they've evolved over centuries of use and their benefits have been well documented—and also because they explicitly aim to reduce or eliminate the conditioning effect of samskaras and vasanas. But it should be said that effective physical and breathing practices have been developed in other cultures as well—China's *tai chi* and *qigong*, for example—and by fitness experts, psychologists, and healthcare practitioners in the modern West. They constitute another set of options that some find worthwhile to consider.

Now let's turn our attention to meditation, which has long been considered the cornerstone of a productive sadhana.

Once upon a time, only spiritual seekers on the fringes of society had heard about meditation, and those pioneers had few opportunities to learn how to do it. Then The Beatles took up Transcendental Meditation, scientists did experiments and published their findings, doctors and therapists started recommending meditation, and the floodgates opened. Other venerable techniques surfaced, while new ones were introduced by both opportunists and serious experts, and now there are more varieties of meditation than breakfast cereals in the marketplace. This is a blessing for humanity. Inevitably, however, along with mainstreaming comes erroneous information and a good deal of confusion.

To begin with, meditation techniques are not all the same. That should be obvious, but the various methods are frequently treated as if they were six of one and half dozen of the other. This defies logic. Why would different techniques produce the same results? Similar maybe, but certainly not identical, as is often assumed.

In recent years, the confusion has been exacerbated by a babel of careless language. The word "contemplative," for example, is often applied to practices that don't involve contemplation in the usual sense of the word, i.e., reflecting on the meaning of a phrase or concept. They might have nothing to do with discursive thinking at all. Similarly, some practices labeled "prayer," such as Centering Prayer, which is popular among many Christians, are not remotely what comes to mind when we think of people praying, i.e., on their knees petitioning the Almighty. In fact, they're more like eastern meditative practices in that they're meant to take our awareness beyond words to intimate communion with the Divine.

Most confusing of all, though, because of the popularity of Buddhist practices and their secularized alternatives, "mindfulness" is commonly used interchangeably with "meditation." One gets conflated with the other, and both terms are used as an umbrella for every practice that turns the attention inward and leads to relaxation. As a result, something called mindfulness might be more of a meditation practice, and something called meditation might be more of a mindfulness practice. But, if mindfulness means remaining mindful of, or focused on, an object of attention, then meditation might more accurately be called mind*empty*ness.

If you're now more confused than you were three paragraphs ago, just remember the central point: regardless of what they're called, meditative methods differ in many ways. For example, some have religious overtones and some are purely secular. Some are guided, some are self-administered. Some involve mantras, some the breath, some a visualized object, some an area in the body, and some no object of attention at all. The factor I find most salient, however, is the degree of effort required.

Imagine a spectrum or continuum with, at one extreme, methods that demand rigorous mind control. Moving toward the other end of the spectrum, we find less strenuous techniques that nevertheless require a certain amount of effort to keep the mind focused on an object. The degree of control required continues to lessen as we pass through the center of the continuum, and eventually we come to methods that emphasize *relinquishing* control. Less and less effort is called for, and more and more ease is encouraged. Finally, we arrive at effortlessness. Each method has its own value, but the differences in both practice and outcome can be considerable.

Based on my experience and research, the more effortless the better. Methods that require rigorous concentration or strenuous attempts to silence the mind can lead to frustration and sometimes headache-inducing strain. In the context of ongoing supervision, that risk may be worth taking. But for solitary at-home practice, it might be ill-advised. The more salient point, however, is that less effort generally leads to more benefit. This seems counterintuitive to Americans who are accustomed to the "no pain, no gain" school of fitness and the "nose-to-the-grindstone" school of success, where anything worth having requires hard work.

Meditation is a different category of endeavor. It's governed by something akin to the principal of least action in physics, which asserts that the path an object will take between two configurations is the one that requires the least action. In other words, nature always chooses the most effort-free option. Similarly, in meditation, nature's direct path from the busy surface of the mind to the quiet depths is the one that demands the least effort.

Why is this so? Because a strenuous attempt to restrain the frisky monkey mind will agitate instead of calm. It's like pressing on the gas pedal and hitting the brake at the same time. Effort-free meditation practices are rooted in the understanding that the mind doesn't have to be tamed; it just has to be allowed to do what it naturally does, which is to seek contentment. And the ultimate contentment is found in the innermost core of Being, which knows no disturbance and whose nature is bliss. Want to clear a muddy pond? Do nothing, just allow the mud to settle. Want to stop a pot of boiling water from bubbling? Just lower the flame and wait. In the same way, meditators experience peaceful contentment when they stop forcing the mind to do something and just allow it to settle. It's letting nature lead the way.

Ah, but meditating with minimal effort doesn't mean just sitting around doing nothing (which has its own value). Method is required, and instruction is recommended.

The best bet is to find a well trained, experienced teacher, preferably one certified by a reputable organization. The choices are plentiful, so discernment is a must. Whether you prefer a technique taught in a secular context or one from a venerable spiritual tradition, there is so much variation that it's wise to seek out recommendations, preferably from people you can rely on more than a Yelp reviewer.

Once you decide to experiment with a practice (or combination of practices), give peace a chance. Don't rush to judgment. Keep it up long enough to make a proper evaluation. It can take a while for the peace one experiences during practice to palpably carry over into active life. And don't expect every minute spent in meditation to be blissful. It won't be: there will be periods of restlessness and periods of boredom, and times when disturbing thoughts arise. But when the session is over, you should feel more relaxed and more at peace than you were before you started.

That said, the rubber meets the road in daily life. An effective repertoire of practices should make it far more likely that the seeds you sow will reap good karmic fruit. So, look for evidence. Has your overall quality of life been upgraded? Are you calmer in times of stress? Do you have more clarity of mind? Are you less prone to anger, anxiety, fear, and depression? More likely to respond to others with loving-kindness? Are you making better choices? Are good things happening? That's how you know if you're onto something good and your karmic graph is trending upward.

And now, an important caveat: *practice does not make perfect.*

I remember how stunned I was when, three months into my life as a devoted meditator, certain aspects of my life went up in flames. The initial transformation had been so remarkable that I convinced myself that every day would get better and better. Imagine my surprise when I suddenly seemed to be going in reverse. But that's life. That's karma. That's the way it is on the long and winding road of transformation. In retrospect, I realized that I'd handled the upheaval better than I would have in the past, and I'd regained my equilibrium more quickly—proof that I *had* progressed, only not exactly the way I'd imagined. To paraphrase Martin Luther King, Jr., the arc of the karmic universe is long, but it bends toward goodness—if you bend it that way.

As I've argued throughout this chapter, one good way to bend it is with spiritual practices. That makes setting aside time for sadhana a wise investment, not a luxury or a religious imperative. I think of it as necessary maintenance, a routine like showering and brushing one's teeth, or programming a computer to scan for viruses when you boot up. But it's not a panacea. Spiritual progress is more of a roller coaster than a cable car straight to the pinnacle. The seeds of karma don't get burned up all at once. There are far too many of those deep impressions for one thing, and the fire of sadhana may not be hot enough to roast some of them. Think of it this way. Some impressions are like dust, easily blown or wiped away. Others are a bit grimy, but removable with a little effort. Still others need more vigorous scrubbing or special tools and cleansers. And some are like toxic waste; they'll be there a long time and have to be conscientiously managed.

And don't forget, there are always karmic waves on the way; they started rolling toward you a long time ago, and nothing is going to stop them. Things you don't like will happen. In fact, some observers claim that spiritual practices can *accelerate* the karmic process, much as paying extra at the post office gets your package delivered overnight instead of two weeks later. The idea is that, since the ultimate goal is to clear out all traces of karmic baggage, one reward of spiritual progress is to get it over with faster, with temporary disturbances being a small price to pay for the ultimate freedom. Perhaps this explains why it's not uncommon to see a conscientious practitioner make swift immediate progress only to get whacked, seemingly out of the blue, by a painful upheaval. Teachers have told such people that they are fortunate to have resolved some karma that was due to arrive later and more destructively. Whether that is actually true or just a clever teaching tool to ameliorate a student's dismay is anyone's guess.

In any event, don't be shocked if you go through a stretch of hell after everything seemed heavenly. Above all, don't conclude that your sadhana has been a waste of time. Your practices will no doubt help you manage the impact of those upheavals with a measure of grace, and you're likely to rebound faster than you would have before.

Adding to Your Repertoire

Don't be surprised if, like most spiritual aspirants, you realize one day that your sadhana routine needs to be re-evaluated and modified like an investment portfolio. Alternatively, you might find that your practices are working splendidly but feel nevertheless that you stand to benefit from supplementing them. To return to our previous analogies, we don't just run anti-virus programs; we attend to our computers in other ways as well. We blow the dust from our keyboards; we update our programs; we back up our work; we delete apps we no longer need. Why not take the same approach to sadhana by enlisting other modalities in the ongoing effort to upgrade your karma?

If you're engaged with a religious tradition, or if you think of the Divine as having a form, a personality, or a presence with which you can communicate, consider making prayer a regular practice. Not as a bargaining chip for a deity who's some kind of potentate, but as a contemplative practice that plants seeds of good karma in your psyche. The humility that accompanies deep, sincere prayer is, in itself, a form of healing; it lifts us out of our egos. Prayer comes in many styles other than pleading for something we want, e.g., praising, questioning, thanking. I've always liked author Anne Lamott's pithy formulation of three essential prayers: help, thanks, and wow. Perhaps there's a form that suits you.

Similarly, many find that singing devotional songs or chanting in traditional styles is transformative. Every tradition has a musical repertoire to choose from. In India, mantra chanting is a venerable science of sound, and the call-and-response version known as *kirtan* has become quite popular in the West. "Chanting mantras works directly on all types of karma, helping to overcome what may have been created inadvertently or ignorantly in this life or some past life," wrote the late mantra expert, Thomas Ashley-Farrand. He further explains, "The vibration produced by chanting mantra begins to alter our inner condition, both physically and spiritually, and to break down energy patterns stored in the subtle body."[62] No such claims have been made for singing hymns in English, or chanting in Hebrew or Latin, but individuals have found those practices to be highly beneficial. At the very least, traditional devotion can lift the heart and soothe the soul.

What about spending time with spiritual companions? Being part of a congregation has long been a central component of religious life in every culture. *Sangha* (spiritual community or assembly) is considered so important in Buddhism that it's one-third of the Threefold Refuge or Triple Gem (as noted in chapter 5, the others are the Buddha and the Dharma). You may not be the joining type, but most communities allow for different levels of engagement; chances are you can find a comfortable way to benefit from camaraderie. In fact, some research indicates that community is the main reason Western worshippers show up even if they don't believe the official doctrines. That said, if solitary practices are more to your liking, why not spend time reading sacred texts—not just to gather information, but to sink into, wallow in, contemplate, and absorb spiritual teachings with the heart?

These are just some ways to fortify our spiritual lives and upgrade our karma. But why disregard secular opportunities? Any art form can be healing if approached in the right way. Every friendship can be sacred if it's allowed to be. Every tree and flower can be an agent of transformation if we're open to it. And there are useful therapeutic interventions for stubborn habits, self-defeating patterns, and repeated mistakes that spring from past traumas and conditioning—those deep impressions that cling to the unconscious like lint. If talking therapy or psychoanalysis don't appeal to you, there are other methods, such as cognitive therapy and somatic therapy that might. As mentioned earlier, it is no longer difficult to find therapists who respect the spiritual quest and might even take concerns about karma seriously.

In the end, it's important to remember that everything we

do and everything we experience, whether or not we consciously invited it, produces impressions and therefore affects our karma. That goes not only for traumatic and painful experiences but the joyful and the sublime as well. An impression is embedded every time we're hugged or kissed on the cheek; every time our hearts swell at a song or a sunset or the smile of a baby; every time we feel a wave of love or gratitude; every time someone praises us or treats us kindly or thanks us for praising them or treating them kindly. The task is to disempower the impressions that lead to regrettable speech and action, and to elevate those that stimulate loving feelings, healthy goals, harmonious speech, and virtuous action. Therefore, it makes sense to evaluate every aspect of our lives for its karmic impact and to do our best to piece together a Good Karma Lifestyle.

Lifestyle Balance

One framework for developing a harmonious, karmically beneficial way of life is the Vedic concept of the three *gunas*. In this model, all of manifest creation—the entire domain of karma—is governed by the interaction of three subtle qualities, aka forces, energies, or tendencies, called gunas. They are:

Sattva—characterized by goodness, serenity, harmony, wisdom, truth, happiness, purity, luminosity, beauty.

Rajas—characterized by passion, action, motion, heat, vitality, desire, creativity, restlessness.

Tamas—characterized by heaviness, inertia, ignorance, rest, lethargy, dullness, apathy, impurity, decay.

These vivid images from the animal kingdom might be helpful in remembering the differences among gunas: sattva = swan, rajas = tiger, tamas = sloth.[63]

Theoretically, the gunas interact in an infinite number of combinations to shape every object, person, and event throughout space and time. Understanding them is considered so valuable as a guide for living that the Bhagavad Gita devotes a number of verses to explaining how the gunas manifest in everything from rituals to work to food to speech. It amounts to this: move toward sattva. reduce excessive rajas, minimize tamas. The more sattvic our behavior, and the more sattvic the forces that influence us, the better our karma.

For example, the foods we consume. Drawing from various Gita translations (ch. 17, v. 8-10), sattvic foods are fresh, mild, flavorful, tasty, agreeable, nourishing, and hearty. Rajasic foods are bitter, acidic, sour, pungent, astringent, spicy, and hot. Tamasic foods are stale, impure, rotten, tasteless, overcooked, and lacking in nutrition. Same with beverages: milk is considered sattvic, coffee rajasic, strong alcohol tamasic.

As another example, here is the Gita's breakdown of the gunas in the workplace (ch. 18, v. 23-25). Sattvic work is performed with enthusiasm and fortitude, in accord with one's duties and responsibilities, and without egotism or selfish attachment to personal reward. Rajasic work is motivated by personal desire, pride, lust, or craving for reward, and is performed with exertion, strain, and toil. Tamasic work is motivated by ignorance or delusion, and is performed lazily, sluggishly, deceitfully, wastefully, and heedless of the harm caused to others.

Keeping the qualities of the gunas in mind, it becomes possible to make lifestyle choices aimed at increasing sattva. Which music, movies, and reading material are most soul-nourishing, for example? Not that we need to abstain from rocking out to rajasic tunes, or to eschew rajasic action movies, but perhaps to enjoy such pleasures in a discerning way. Maybe start favoring entertainment that elevates, inspires, and soothes, while reducing the consumption of those that drain our energy and leave us feeling inert, foggy, or depressed. The same goes for jobs, relationships, neighborhoods, vacations, newscasts, sports, social gatherings, business associates, social media sites, organizations, hobbies, and everything else in our lives. By elevating sattva we plant more positive impressions in the mind, and that, as we've seen, leads to karmically auspicious thought and action.

That said, a caveat: *Don't overdo it.* In general, the more sattva the better, but we need the energy, drive, and passion of rajas too. And tamas isn't all bad either; it can be grounding and stabilizing, and it gets us to lie down and sleep when we need it. A proper understanding of the three gunas should lead to balance and harmony, but unfortunately, seekers of purity often mess up their lives by going too far too quickly. It's axiomatic, for instance, that being a vegetarian is more sattvic, and better karmically, than dining on murdered animals. But is that necessarily true for every individual? What if your body requires some animal protein, as I was told by an Ayurvedic doctor who was himself a strict vegetarian? What if—and I've seen this many times—being an uncompromising vegan makes you so spaced out and irritable that other aspects of your life are compromised? Point of fact: Hitler was a vegetarian and the Dalai Lama is not. What does that tell us?

I've known people who dedicated so much time and energy to purification that their families felt neglected and their home lives were toxic. I've seen people quit jobs abruptly because their workplace wasn't sattvic enough only to suffer the stress of being unemployed and broke. I've seen couples allow only sattvic entertainment in their homes only to have their kids sneak around doing wild and risky things. As Ralph Waldo Emerson put it, "Moderation in all things, especially moderation."

Lines Across the Water

One way of envisioning the long-term karmic impact of sadhana and sattvic living is with a metaphor I learned in the early days of my spiritual path. For most of us, the impressions that lodge in our systems through experience are like lines chopped into stone by an axe. They have observable consequences, and they last a very long time. As our practices deepen and we advance spiritually, impressions become more like lines carved in firm soil, visible but less so than the axe-on-stone variety, and much shorter-lived. Further along the evolutionary path, impressions become more like lines drawn in mud, then sand, then, lo and behold, like a stick passing through water, and finally, for rare birds, a hand gesturing in the air, evanescent.

Most of us would be happy to reach the line-in-mud stage in this lifetime, and sand would be peachy indeed. As for water and air, that's the status of souls who are firmly anchored in the Divine, beyond the winds of karma. For them, presumably, agency belongs to cosmic intelligence, or God for those who prefer theistic language. As noted earlier, the veracity of that premise may be unprovable since awakening is, by definition, an inner state and therefore not observable by ordinary means and not measurable (at least not yet). As an aspirational model, though, it's no less useful than a high school basketball player learning from Caitlin Clark videos. As long as we're realistic, descriptions of life on the mountaintop can serve as a barometer of our own progress. As we trudge up the trail, the qualities attributed to enlightenment begin to appear, however dimly, like a recognizable face emerging in a child's drawings or the Caitlin wannabe's jump shot swishing the nets more consistently.

Does the impact of this or that bit of karma feel less like an axe on stone and more like a spoon through sand or a twig whipping through the air? Do you seem to be driven less by compulsion and conditioning and more from genuine free choice? Are you less and less needy, greedy, selfish, and constrained? Are you moving through life with less friction—"more gliding than colliding" as one guru put it? Do people seem friendlier and more cooperative? Are things working out as you'd hoped? Do small gifts and unexpected opportunities show up? Do you find yourself feeling happy for no discernible reason? Those are reliable signs that you're decluttering old piles of negative karma and creating less of it day to day.

Another criterion: are you finding it easier and more natural to make karmically wise choices? In some circumstances, such as major life decisions, we might reason our way to right action. On the everyday level, however, there's little time for fact-gathering and analysis, so we have to feel our way to right action. We have to rely on intuition. And one thing we can assert with reasonable certainty is that deep spiritual practice enhances intuition. It defogs the mind and clears the way for the subtle signals of knowing. Dean Sluyter summed it up nicely: "Most people who've done serious meditative practice for some time notice that as our perception grows clearer, we see more clearly what's right or wrong to do in each moment without having to think much about it. Doing right gets easier, and, perhaps more profoundly, doing wrong gets harder."[64]

8
Ties That Bind

"Let us not talk of karma, but simply of responsibility toward the whole world." *–H.H. the Dalai Lama*

When I told people I was working on this book, a surprising number were happy to hear it because, as one of them put it, "If more people believe in karma, the world will be a better place."

That would seem to be a reasonable assertion. Why wouldn't belief in an inviolable system of cause and effect lead to more virtuous behavior? Why wouldn't it make people less apt to do harm to others? After all, it's pure self-interest to avoid the consequences of wrongdoing and enjoy the rewards of honorable conduct. The second-century Buddhist sage Nagarjuna seems to have agreed: "How can those who consider how the fruit of helpful and harmful deeds ripens persist in their selfishness for even a single moment?"

Clearly, it's only logical to assume that widespread belief in karma would multiply the acts of generosity and kindness in the world. Paul Brunton, who spent considerable time in India, is one of many who predicted as much. "The ethics of the future," he wrote, "will be founded on rational understanding of the power of karma, the law of personal responsibility; and this will lead to right restraint on conduct." Similarly, Rudolf Steiner, the

Austrian mystic who founded the Anthroposophical Society in the early twentieth century, felt that an understanding of karma and reincarnation was essential for the future of Western civilization. "The feeling of responsibility will be intensified to a degree that was formerly impossible," he said of such a development, "and other moral insights will necessarily follow." Steiner also made this assertion: "If this idea of karma is put earnestly into effect a significant change will be brought about, not in methods of education only but in the whole of life."

It's certainly tempting, and not entirely irrational, to imagine that the adoption of a karmic ethos would usher in a new era of natural morality. It would motivate upright behavior and radically reduce the quotient of greed, cruelty, hatred, duplicity, and other caustic traits. It would revolutionize how we educate and raise our children. Law enforcement would change dramatically. The need to regulate business would virtually disappear. Resources could be redirected to socially constructive purposes. With peace assured, the United Nations could focus on other needs, and the International Criminal Court could shut its doors.

Well, history would like a word.

Haven't Judeo-Christian cultures attempted something very much like that? Centuries of preaching in churches, synagogues, and mosques convinced the masses that if they behaved in accord with a particular moral code, they would earn favor with the Almighty and be handsomely rewarded, possibly in this earthly life but surely afterward and for all eternity. With even greater power of conviction, clerical authorities had their constituents quaking in their boots in fear that their sins would doom them to a flaming oven of pain without a chance of parole. Seems like a perfect formula for inculcating good behavior. How did it work out?

If we've learned anything from Western history it's that piety, Bible worship, and afterlife insurance policies not only did not prevent atrocities, in many instances they instigated them. It can be argued that belief in karma is more likely to get people to shape up than would belief in an omnipotent magistrate with a galaxy-sized gavel. At a glance, it does seem that cultures in which karma is broadly accepted have been more peaceful and more neighborly over the centuries than those shaped by the Abrahamic religions. But a closer look at Asian history evens the score a good deal. And while the sacred texts of the Indic traditions have inspired and guided millions of righteous souls around the world, they also count villains among their fans. Some of Hitler's henchmen were fond of the Bhagavad Gita, for instance, and reportedly, so is leading Trump-whisperer Steve Bannon.

Clearly, karma is as vulnerable to abuse as other beliefs, philosophies, and empirical insights. Indeed, bending the meaning of karma in a self-serving way has proved a quite useful strategy for keeping marginalized people in check; it's hard to find a more expedient way to justify exploitation than "It's their karma." It's not hard, after all, for the wealthy to argue that their privilege was earned in past lives while the destitute are merely paying the price of their previous wrongdoing. I've even heard it argued that raising taxes on the rich to fund programs for the disadvantaged is a misguided attempt to nullify karma. How different is that from saying social inequities are God's will?

At the same time, maintaining a belief in karma does seem to make a difference in individual lives, and as a shaper of conscience it might be more persuasive to the modern mind than belief in a pearly gates accounting system. It is plain to me, based on my personal experience and dozens of conversations, that something changes when one accepts that karmic law is real. In fact, something changes even if one only accepts that karma *might* be real. You start to factor into your thinking that whatever you do will, or at least *could*, ricochet back in a meaningful way, even if the nature and timing of the payoff can't be predicted. The conviction—even a strong suspicion—that our actions have consequences adds or subtracts from the weight we assign to our choices, and that can be enough to tip the scales in the right direction. In my experience (amplified by people I've interviewed), it's as though, at moments of decision, I felt a tap on the shoulder and heard a whisper, "Don't forget about karma." I've compared it to being a child who's not sure Santa is real but, when faced with whether to be naughty or nice, remembers the Christmas tune and figures he'd better be good for goodness sake.

Suppose you know that something you're tempted to do is ethically or morally wrong, but you also know that you'll gain in the short run from doing it and there's very little chance anyone will ever know what you've done. Absent karma, you might go ahead with it. But now, instead, you hesitate because there's a good chance that if you do that wrong thing something undesirable will happen down the road. The same is true on the positive side of the ledger. Say you have the opportunity to perform a kindness that no one will know about. The possibility that you might derive karmic benefit by going ahead with it, aside from feeling good about yourself, can turn a maybe into a yes. In short, as one of my sources put it, "When I think about it, karma often changes what I do or don't do."

Ah, but "When I think about it" is a huge caveat and one of the main reasons we ought to be circumspect when assessing the societal impact of belief in karma. As Christopher Isherwood put it, "The concept of karma is only valuable insofar as it reminds us of the extraordinary importance of our every thought and action, and of our immense responsibility toward each other."[65] Even those whose belief in karma is resolute—a built-in feature of their software, so to speak, no installation required—don't necessarily think about it before they act, especially if doing so might be inconvenient. Much of the time, we react to events, make spontaneous choices, and follow our guts. We run on automatic like driverless cars.

We can only conclude that, while belief is important, exactly how potent it is in real life situations depends on the capacity of one's awareness and the quality of one's heart. We all know how easy it is for the best of intentions to be overwhelmed by the power of self-deception, egotism, and desire. As Duryodhana, the main antagonist in the Mahabharata, laments, "I know what is dharma, yet I feel no inclination to follow it; I know what is adharma [not dharma], yet I cannot desist from it. I do everything as some Being seated in my heart directs me to do."

Consciousness and Conscience

A consistent tenet of the Hindu and Buddhist teachers who came to the West was that the advancement of consciousness through spiritual practice is invariably accompanied by concomitant progress in moral and ethical behavior. According to this thesis, the palpable benefits of practice—acute perception, a tender heart, attunement to the subtle currents of nature—lead spontaneously to right action. The logic is quite convincing, and the improved lives of practitioners provides a certain amount of validation. In the previous chapter, in fact, I presented a modified version of this proposition, but I was careful to qualify it by suggesting that spiritual practice *improves the odds* of karma-friendly behavior, not that it guarantees it. That's because we've learned the hard way that even methods that effectively accelerate psychospiritual growth offer no air-tight guarantee of virtue.

As originally presented, the dynamic was held to be automatic: in a straight line of evolutionary progress, right action will grow as consciousness grows, like the boxcars on a train advance at the same speed as the locomotive. From that assumption, it followed that those who reach the highest levels of development—call it awakening, liberation, enlightenment or whatever your favorite term is—are ipso facto supremely moral and ethical beings. What else could they be if the locomotive had reached the pinnacle, hauling the boxcars of egoless compassion, love, and kindness right along with it? Because enlightened beings are perfectly attuned to divine intelligence, the reasoning goes, their actions necessarily reflect absolute goodness—what the religious would call the will of God. Maharishi Mahesh Yogi was a prominent voice for this perspective. "[I]t is possible to adjust the whole stream of life so that every action performed is naturally good or right," he wrote, adding, "Since there is a way to regulate one's life by the laws of nature, then all one's thought, speech and action can produce an influence in accordance with these laws working for the maintenance and evolution of all things." In this way, he asserted, "all karma becomes a karma of absolute righteousness."[66]

Based on the evidence, however, the formula appears to have been overstated. There is no doubt that the correlation between spiritual development and right action is stronger than skeptics might think it is, but it's also not as airtight as gurus and devotees believed it to be—or hoped it would be. Overall, spiritual growth tends to amplify the best in us and diminish the worst. But there does not appear to be a one-to-one correspondence; practice alone does not make perfection (if there is such a thing in the first place). The proof of that conclusion was, ironically, provided by the very gurus who propagated the notion that anything an enlightened person does is cosmically righteous even if it doesn't appear that way to lesser evolved eyes. The assumption of moral perfection granted venerated gurus extraordinary latitude when it came to their own behavior, and, needless to say, many took advantage of it.

When I was researching my book, *American Veda,* I learned to my dismay that there had been more guru scandals in the 1960s and 70s than I'd realized. Most were sexual, some were financial, others were about power abuse, but what they had in common was credulity on the part of earnest devotees: "If the master does it, by definition it's right action." My chapter on the topic was the shortest in the book and the hardest to write. It also drew the most extreme reactions. On the one hand, "How could you say such terrible things about my peerless guru?" (Never mind the evidence.) On the other hand, "You were too kind to that reprobate."

Sad to say, the ensuing years brought additional revelations about past transgressions. New scandals erupted as well, involving not only Indian gurus but also Buddhist teachers (both Asian and American-born), as well as yoga instructors, independent spiritual teachers, and to the shock of parishioners, mainstream clergy—and, it is safe to assume, every one of the perpetrators believed in karma or another form of cosmic justice. The disclosures gave rise not only to trauma and rage, but to considerable handwringing, painful reckonings, agonizing healing, and vigorous attempts to understand the phenomenon and prevent future occurrences.[67]

Out of the personal struggles and rigorous analyses that followed came the unavoidable conclusion that the "spontaneous right action" model of flawless saints and saints-in-the-making simply does not hold up to scrutiny. Either the theory that enlightened awareness brings with it impeccable morality is flawed or enlightenment itself has to be redefined. Sorting this out is an ongoing project, but it seems safe to conclude that spiritual growth—or, as some prefer to call it, the development of consciousness—is not a locomotive that pulls all meritorious traits behind it, but only one line of human development among many. To be sure, it's a special developmental line, and a powerful one, but it's not the master switch that, when lit, illuminates all other areas of life equally. The model of separate lines of development has gained considerable currency in the years since it was first proposed by integral philosopher Ken Wilber.

It's also only logical to conclude that *all* human beings, even the presumably self-realized, are shaped by their karmic histories as long as they retain bodies and personalities. The exalted ones too must have shadow elements lurking unseen in the unconscious. Therefore, it's safe to assume that they ought to be guided by moral and ethical standards, in the spirit of the legendary

Buddhist master Padmasambhava, who said, "Although my awareness is as vast as the sky, my attention to karma is as fine as a grain of barley flour."[68] He would probably have agreed that even anointed spiritual masters should be held accountable when they fall short of accepted ethical standards.

So, what can we conclude about the social implications of karma doctrine becoming broadly accepted?

I believe we've established three things: 1) widespread belief in karma can go only so far in shaping a better future for humanity, 2) merely coaxing people to live up to ethical codes and moral precepts is also insufficient, and 3) the widespread adoption of proven methods of growth and transformation would be a big step forward but would not be enough by itself. That leads us to ponder what the world would be like if all three of those elements—a persuasive educational effort about the laws of karma, rigorous moral and ethical training, and widespread application of effective development tools—were to be implemented on a broad scale. One can only hope that our collective karma will permit such an experiment.

No Karma Is an Island

I was working on the first draft of this book when Donald Trump was elected U.S. President for the second time. Like just about everyone I knew, I found it distressing in the extreme that such an extravagantly flawed human being could once again ascend to the heights of power. Since karma was on my mind at the time, I reached out to some scholars of Hinduism and Buddhism, thinking they might have some wisdom to share. I asked a simple question: "What does the election say about America's collective karma?" Here's a sample of their replies:

"It doesn't say anything good."

"Native American genocide. Human enslavement. Need I go on?"

"That we need to learn the lessons his presence will bring to us. Unfortunately, those lessons will come with a cost."

"We have to peer into our collective shadow and face squarely what lurks there."

"We're experiencing the bad karma of embracing materialistic values and selfishness over compassion and spirituality."

By the time you read this, the world will know a lot more about the karmic impact of that election and the administration it ushered in. What's of most interest, though, is the elaboration I received from some of the people I queried. Some expanded on the meaning of collective karma while others questioned whether collective karma actually exists. The latter came as a surprise. I had taken for granted what I'd heard over the years, which was that we all partake not only of our individual karma but also of family karma, community karma, national karma, and the karma of other groupings to which we belong, such as religion, ethnicity, race, business, and voluntary associations from reading groups to civic organizations. Not to mention the shared karma of people who come together seemingly by chance, whether in communal joy at a concert, a ball game, or a political rally, or in the shared heartbreak of a mass murder, a terrorist attack, or an earthquake, flood, or other so-called Acts of God.

It turns out that the existence of group karma is by no means a settled issue, either among scholars or within Hindu and Buddhist lineages. In fact, those who affirm the existence of collective karma might well be in the minority.

The arguments against the idea center on how to define a karma-producing entity. "Morality, responsibility, and their consequences are rooted in consciousness," a Buddhist correspondent told me. "Without consciousness and free will, there is no karma. And only individuals have consciousness; larger entities do not." Another scholar concurred from a Hindu perspective: "My sense is that karma is possessed only by jivas"—what the West might call individual souls—"and therefore there is no such thing as collective karma, per se." Swami Medhananda, a monk in the Ramakrishna Order with a Ph.D. from the University of California, Berkeley, concurs with that view. In his own book on karma he writes, "All classical and most modern Hindu thinkers held that karma pertains strictly to the individual soul."[69] Concluding otherwise, he told me, "presupposes a group soul as a separate ontological entity," something only small number of thinkers have done. Among the notable exceptions was the eminent philosopher and historian Ananda Coomaraswamy, who said that karma "holds as much for groups and communities as for individuals," and Sri Aurobindo, who wrote:

> What I sow in this hour, is reaped by my posterity for several generations and we can then call it the karma of the family. What the men of today as community or people resolve upon and execute, comes back with a blessing or a sword upon the future of their race when they themselves have passed away and are no longer there to rejoice or to suffer; and that we can speak of as the karma of the nation. Mankind as a whole too has a karma; what it wrought in its past, will shape its future destiny; individuals seem only to be temporary units of human thought, will, nature who act according to the compulsion of the soul in humanity and disappear; but the karma of the race which they have helped to form continues through the centuries, the millenniums, the cycles.[70]

Those who oppose the notion of group karma point out that even collective decisions are made by individuals, and only individuals reap the consequences of those decisions. Moreover, they note, reincarnation is a necessary component of any theory of karma, and only individual souls (jivas) get reborn; groups as such do not. Buddhists reject the idea of individual jivas, but their arguments for and against group karma are quite similar to those of the Hindu experts. Summing it up, the Indian scholar Y. (Yuvraj) Krishan writes, "The concept of a 'social soul' of various groups and having common stock of karmas is alien to Indian religious thought. In any case there is no 'social soul' which is liable to death and rebirth."[71]

In our conversation, however, Swami Medhananda allowed that the notion of collective karma can be "heuristically helpful as a metaphor." I find that caveat helpful. If, strictly speaking, group karma doesn't exist, then something very much like it clearly does. Call it group karma adjacent.

It seems obvious that human groupings take on a coherent character of their own, and that character is more than the sum of its parts—and by parts I mean the karmic dynamics of each individual in the group. Some kind of alchemy is at play, just as it is when carrots, onions, and other veggies become one soup even as the ingredients retain their individual shapes, colors, and flavors. There's a reason why sociologists study group dynamics and psychologists analyze family patterns, not just the psyches of each member. We speak of team chemistry in sports, and of corporate culture in business, and we reward leaders who know how to enhance those subtle undercurrents to get better results. Similarly, diplomats and seasoned travelers are conversant about the national traits of different countries.

Whether such phenomena qualify as collective karma is a matter of definition, but it's inarguable that the actions taken by every individual in a group affect the other members in varying degrees, and, it should be emphasized, individuals react to collective events according to their personal karmic portfolio. It can also be said that individual actions have an impact on the group as a whole, and some decisions are *group* decisions, made on behalf of the entity itself. A family decides to go on a road trip together. A CEO changes the company's marketing strategy. A mayor launches an infrastructure project. The effects of those decisions will affect every family member, employee, and citizen, as well as the family, company, and town *as a whole*.

Does that not come close to being group karma?

The same can be said of all groupings, from tiny ones like a romantic couple to big and powerful ones like nations. Suppose I receive separate birthday presents from each member of a nuclear family. My response will obviously be different than if I'd received one gift on behalf of the entire family. If the government of Chile changes a significant economic policy, every Chilean citizen will be affected, as will the inhabitants of countries who trade with Chile. If a similar decision is made by the Chinese government, not only the inhabitants of China but every nation on earth and the planet itself stand to be affected. If I buy stock in a company, I'll celebrate the gains and lament the losses like all the other stockholders, except we'll each gain or lose a different sum. If I go into business with four partners, with each of us investing an equal amount, we'll all enjoy the same profit or incur the same loss—and so will the business entity as such. When a sports team wins or loses, the results are felt by every player, fan, and staff member, and the organization as a whole benefits or suffers.

In every one of those examples, each affected person experiences the outcomes in their own unique way, according to their karmic histories, because as Herman Hesse wrote in his novel *Demian,* everyone "represents the unique, the very special and always significant and remarkable point at which the world's phenomena intersect, only once in this way and never again." But, at the same time, isn't some kind of group karma—a karmic network so to speak—in play along with all the individual karmas? If, strictly speaking, it's incorrect to refer to, say, a Beatles karma apart from the karmas of John, Paul, George, and Ringo, then I for one would rather be incorrect than give up a perfectly useful metaphor to describe a perfectly obvious phenomenon.

The Perplexing Problem of Mass Catastrophes

It would not be surprising if your response to this exploration is to ask: What about people who are thrown together for no apparent reason except to suffer some miserable fate? For example, the victims of a hurricane, earthquake, or wildfire that destroys a vast swath of inhabited territory; the concertgoers at the Las Vegas venue when a gunman emptied a thousand rounds into the jam-packed crowd; the doomed souls who happened to be in the World Trade Center on 9/11, or on the hijacked airplanes. Flipping the karmic scenario, what about the "lucky" ones who slept through the alarm on September 11, 2001, or took the day off because of a doctor's appointment? Such collectives are worlds apart from the bonds of a nuclear family, a neighborhood, a corporation, or a nation. And what about large subcultures—Jews, Palestinians, African Americans, et al—whose diverse members are spread out over time and space and are linked only by categories devised by humans, and yet suffer as a group from bigotry and oppression? What about historical abominations like the Holocaust, chattel slavery, and colonization?

These are the questions that inevitably arise in discussions of collective karma. The commentators I've come across agree on one fundamental point: assuming that karma is real, every single one of the victims was in that specific place at that specific time for reasons connected to their past, and that past necessarily includes previous incarnations. I have yet to find a convincing explanation for exactly what those souls might have done in the past that led them to those fateful situations, or what actually might have caused the cataclysm in question—and I don't expect ever to find one. The many attempts by psychics, astrologers, and presumably all-knowing holy figures to fill in the details must be regarded as sheer speculation or the products of facile imaginations. At their worst, the explainers risk coming across as heartless by suggesting—and sometimes stating explicitly—that the victims *deserved* their fates because they must have committed terrible deeds in a previous life. They should know that callous language, like callous actions and callous attitudes, has karmic consequences.

Human atrocities and "acts of God" understandably make rational people dismiss karma as a convenient theory at best and harmful hogwash at worst. For anyone inclined to believe that karma *does* exist, and that the universe is orderly and lawful, the only sensible conclusion is the one we've returned to again and again throughout the book: the intricacies of karma are unfathomable. Remember the analogy of pebbles dropped in a pond, and the difference between following the ripples from one dropped pebble as compared to the colliding waves of ten or twenty pebbles? Well, imagine a whole barrel of pebbles poured into a pond at the same time.

We can't know *why* large collective events happen the way they do. From the perspective of karma, we can only say that nothing is a coincidence. The people affected didn't *cause* the hurricane or the flood or the mass shooter, but karmic currents carried them to that place of calamity at that calamitous moment in time. And every single one of them experienced the event in accord with their own karmic configuration. Karma determined the extent of their injuries, the nature of their traumas, the intensity of their pain and suffering, and whether or not they survived. And for the survivors, the chemistry of free will and karma determined how the disastrous experience affected their lives going forward.

We can let academics sweat the definitions and distinctions. What matters on the playing field of real life is that 1) everything we do affects everyone else in each of our groupings and of every group as a whole, and 2) we are each affected by what every other member does and by everything the collective entity does on behalf of the whole. Setting aside the incomprehensible and the inconceivable—the Holocaust, 9/11, etc.—what we see in ordinary events is that the web of karma has many threads, and the threads multiply and shift with everything we think, say, and do. No one plucks on a thread without feeling the vibration.

Do What You Can

That we're simultaneously separate entities and intricately inseparable—trees in a forest, waves on a sea, grains of sand on a beach, musicians in an orchestra, pick your metaphor—is pure science. "Interconnectedness is fundamental, at all scales," says science educator J.D. Stillwater. "There are no isolated systems." When Neil deGrasse Tyson said that humans are connected to one another biologically, and to the earth chemically, and to the universe atomically, he surely didn't dream of adding *karmically.* To do so would suggest that our actions not only affect one another, they also reverberate and return to impact the actor. Perhaps science, which has already given us the mind-boggling notion of quantum entanglement,[72] will one day discover karmic entanglement as well.

In the meantime, karma remains a metaphysical insight, a doctrine, a belief, a hypothesis, an article of faith, a convincing intuition, or a reasonable deduction. Whatever frame one wishes to place it in, anyone who embraces karma even tentatively is led to an important takeaway. As the Bible says, "To whom much is given, much is required" (Luke 12:48). If you've been able to purchase this book, and you've had the capacity and time to read it, and a comfortable place to read it in, you are among the karmically privileged. You may be troubled. You may be in pain. You may suffer from loss and deprivation and all manner of indignities. But still, in the context of the overall human condition, you are blessed. Much has been given to you.

Among those gifts is this: you know about karma. And anyone who knows anything about karma knows that it is, among other things, a bold and unequivocal assertion of individual responsibility. That means, first and foremost, that we're each responsible for our own actions and their consequences. It also means that we affect the karma of others, both those whom we cherish and untold others we'll never know. Not only that, but we help shape the karma—the fate or destiny, if you prefer that kind of language—of every group of which we're a part, and that same collective impacts us. That goes for small groupings like our families as well as the enormous ones we don't think we're important enough to influence. "You are one of those individuals whose thought and conduct will help to make your nation's karma," wrote Paul Brunton.

But why stop there? Surely each of us affects all other sentient beings, and every object on the planet, and every atom of the planet itself. Even if the karmic seeds we sow yield only a small fruit or two compared to the giant orchards planted by the mighty, we have a responsibility to seed kindness, love, and compassion. We owe it not only to our loved ones, our neighbors, and our fellow citizens, but also to ourselves. That's one of the cool things about karma: it makes a selfless act a selfish act. But there's a catch: since, as we've seen, intention matters a great deal, pretending you mean it simply won't do.

Whether you call it collective karma, or the physics of interconnectedness, or just good citizenship, it is clearly a wise karmic strategy to contribute in some way to the well-being of the larger whole. The world needs evolving individuals who can dip into the depths of their being and pour into the world a measure of the serenity, compassion, love, and insight they find within—and to do so sincerely, humbly, and in full alignment with their own unique dharma. In a previous period of uncertainty and turmoil, the public figure who started out as Professor Richard Alpert and became the spiritual teacher Ram Dass captured the spirit of karmic responsibility: "I've been asked many times whether this is the Aquarian age and it's all just beginning, or if this is Armageddon and this is the end, and I have to admit I don't know. Whichever way it goes, my work is the same. My work is to quiet my mind and open my heart and relieve suffering wherever I find it."

We all do that naturally with the beings we care about—the ones who fit comfortably within our circle of immediate concern. As we evolve and our minds expand and our hearts melt, that circle of concern tends to expand. One of our tasks, therefore, is to not let the circle of kinship stop expanding, but rather to let it swell like a balloon. "How big is your we?" asks Rev. Jim Wallis in *Who Speaks for God?* "Can we expand our vision of community beyond our own skin, family, race, tribe, culture, country, and species? . . . That is both a spiritual and a political question. How we answer it will likely determine our future."

Given the constraints on our time, resources, and influence, what we are able to contribute may seem trivial—a proverbial drop in an ocean of misery. But every ounce of karmic relief delivered with grace and integrity is a difference-maker. As Buddha reportedly said, "Do not overlook tiny good actions, thinking they are of no benefit. Even tiny drops of water in the end will fill a huge vessel."

You'll be drinking from that vessel along with the rest of us, so make your drop sweet and pure.

Notes

[1] The most prominent figures in this category were Sir William Jones (1746-94), Henry Thomas Colebrooke (1765-1837), and Max Müller (1823-1900).

[2] It is also known as the Bengal Renaissance after the province in which it was centered.

[3] Diana L. Eck, *A New Religious America* (HarperCollins, 2001), 95.

[4] Other New Thought groups still in operation include Christian Science, the Unity churches, and Science of Mind (now generally known as Centers for Spiritual Living).

[5] Exact sales figures are unknown but thought to be upward of five million worldwide.

[6] J.D. Salinger, *Nine Stories* (Back Bay Books/Little, Brown and Co., 1948), 287.

[7] "New-Age Beliefs and Practices," YouGov poll, August 18-22, 2022. https://today.yougov.com/health/articles/44581-most-americans-hold-some-new-age-beliefs-poll

[8] He was India's president from 1962 to 1967.

[9] Sri Aurobindo, *Essays in Philosophy and Yoga* (Sri Aurobindo Ashram, 2012), 361.

[10] "New-Age Beliefs and Practices," YouGov poll.

[11] Philip Goff quotes are from his 2017 article, "The Case for Panpsychism," in the magazine *Philosophy Now.*

[12] The four are the Rig, Yajur, Sama, and Atharva, collectively known as the Vedic Samhitas, samhita meaning "collection."

[13] Shrinivas Tilak, *Understanding Karma,* (International Centre for Cultural Studies, 2006), 30-1.

[14] Jeffery Long, *Historical Dictionary of Hinduism* (Scarecrow Press, 2011), 7.

[15] Long, 8.

[16] The Bhagavad Gita and the Brahma Sutras are also considered foundational.

[17] Tilak, 138.

[18] S. Radhakrishnan, *Indian Philosophy* (Oxford University Press, 2008, original publication 1923), Volume 1, 201.

[19] About a thousand years later, something similar would happen with Sikhism.

[20] Radhakrishnan, 298-99.

[21] J. Bruce Long, "The Concepts of Human Action and Rebirth in the *Mahabharata,*" in *Karma and Rebirth in the Indian Traditions,* Wendy Doniger O'Flaherty, ed. (University of California Press, 1980).

[22] Radhakrishnan, 431.

[23] Tilak, 48.

[24] Wendy Doniger O'Flaherty, "Karma and Rebirth in the Vedas and Puranas," in *Karma and Rebirth in the Indian Traditions,* Wendy Doniger O'Flaherty, ed.

[25] Bhagavad Gita, Chapter 2, verse 46.

[26] Swami Prabhavananda and Christopher Isherwood, *How to Know God: The Yoga Aphorisms of Patanjali* (Vedanta Press, 1953), 131.

[27] Radhakrishnan, 265.

[28] From the Buddhist scripture, the *Anguttara Nikaya* (3.72) cited in Traleg Kyabgon, *Karma* (Shambala, 2015), 40.

[29] Paul Brunton, "Karma: The Law of Consequences," Paul Brunton Philosophical Society archive, https://www.paulbrunton.org/publications/miscellaneous-pb-writings/law-of-consequences/.

[30] The interview can be viewed here: https://batgap.com/swamini-brahmaprajnananda-saraswati/. The transcript can be read here: https://batgap.com/swamini-brahmaprajnananda-saraswati-transcript/.

[31] Other meanings include to err and tragic flaw.

[32] James P. McDermott, *Karma and Rebirth in Early Buddhism* in *Karma and Rebirth in Classical Indian Traditions* (University of California Press, 1980), 178.

[33] Santosh Krinsky, Readings in Sri Aurobindo's *Rebirth and Karma* (Lotus Press, 2013), 228.

[34] Maharishi Mahesh Yogi, *Bhagavad Gita: A New Translation and Commentary, Chapters 1-6* (Penguin Books, 1969), 276.
[35] It is also spelled *paticcasamupada.*
[36] Kyabgon, 41.
[37] "The Charge of the Light Brigade," with the passage "Theirs not to make reply / Theirs not to reason why / Theirs but to do and die / Into the valley of Death / Rode the six hundred.
[38] Jack Kornfield, *After the Ecstasy, the Laundry* (Bantam Books, 2000), 132.
[39] Rainer Maria Rilke, *Letters to a Young Poet* (Norton, 1934), 35.
[40] Radhakrishnan, 389.
[41] The nuanced differences between samskaras and vasanas are discussed in chapter seven.
[42] Dean Sluyter, "Sublime Generosity in Charles Dickens's A Christmas Carol," in *Tricycle: The Buddhist Review*, December 19, 2022.
[43] Thich Nhat Hanh, *The Heart of Buddha's Teaching* (Harmony, 1998), 196-7.
[44] Ibid, 198-205.
[45] The remark as been attributed variously to Mel Brooks, Groucho Marx, and George Burns, perhaps others as well.
[46] As translated by Jaganath Carrera, *Inside the Yoga Sutras* (Integral Yoga Publications, 2006), 138.
[47] From the essay *Karma: The Law of Consequences,* https://www.paulbrunton.org/law-of-consequences.php.
[48] Cited in Feuerstein, 245.
[49] Swami Nirviseshananda Tirtha, "Lies That are Necessary," https://www.bhoomananda.org/videos/041-by-swami-nirviseshananda-tirtha-lies-that-are-necessary/
[50] Kim, J.J., Payne, E.S. & Tracy, E.L. Indirect Effects of Forgiveness on Psychological Health Through Anger and Hope: A Parallel Mediation Analysis. *Journal of Religion and Health*, 61, 3729–46 (2022). https://doi.org/10.1007/s10943-022-01518-4
[51] https://www.hopkinsmedicine.org/health/wellness-and-prevention/forgiveness-your-health-depends-on-it.
[52] Cited in the Psychology Today blog, October 8, 2022. https://www.psychologytoday.com/us/blog/what-the-wild-things-are/202210/apologizing-and-making-amends.
[53] Another framework for these layers is that of three *shariras*, or bodies.

Karya sharira is the physical body, identical with annamaya kosha. *Sukshma sharira*, which metaphysicians call the subtle body, consists of the pranamaya, manomaya, and vijnanamaya koshas. *Karana sharira* is the causal body, or anandamaya kosha.

[54] Ellen Langer, *The Mindful Body: Thinking Our Way to Chronic Health* (Ballantine Books, 2023), 39-40.

[55] Sadhguru, *Karma: A Yogi's Guide to Crafting Your Destiny* (Harmony Books, 2021) 26-27.

[56] Thich Nhat Hanh, 51-2.

[57] Leading with Compassion Has Research-Backed Benefits, by Stephen Trzeciak, Anthony Mazzarelli and Emma Seppälä, *Harvard Business Review,* February 27, 2023. https://hbr.org/2023/02/leading-with-compassion-has-research-backed-benefits.

[58] The phrase has been translated in various ways, with, for example, "suppression," or "quieting" instead of "cessation," and "consciousness" in place of "mind-stuff."

[59] In fact, nothing is really united with anything else, since the self and Self were always One and always will be. The difference is, we've now become *aware* of that unity, just as we become aware of sunlight when we lift the window shade.

[60] Maharishi Mahesh Yogi, *The Science of Being and Art of Living* (International SRM Publications, 1963) 48.

[61] Radakrishnan, 359.

[62] Thomas Ashley-Farrand, *Healing Mantras* (Ballantine, 1999), 41 and 49.

[63] Thanks to Robert Mulhall, CEO of the Kripalu Institute for Yoga and Health, for the animal analogs.

[64] Dean Sluyter, *Clear Light, High Society: Sublime Ethics in Virginia Woolf's Mrs. Dalloway,* Tricycle: The Buddhist Review, Feb 8, 2023.

[65] Christopher Isherwood, "What is Vedanta," in *Living Wisdom: Vedanta in the West,* Pravrajika Vrajaprana ed. (Vedanta Press, 1946), 25.

[66] Maharishi Mahesh Yogi, *The Science of Being and Art of Living* (International SRM Publications, 1966), 140-1.

[67] One such effort is the Association for Spiritual Integrity, on whose board I sit as of this writing. The ASI website, https://www.spiritual-integrity.org/, contains up-to-date information about its Honor Code of Ethics and Good Practice and various services.

[68] Thanks to Rick Archer, host of Buddha at the Gas Pump, for supplying that quote.

[69] Swami Medhananda, *Karma and Rebirth in Hinduism* (Cambridge University Press, forthcoming) .

[70] Sri Aurobindo, *Rebirth and Karma* (Lotus Press, 1991), 94-5. Sri Aurobindo used "race" in the broad sense in which the term was understood at the time, as a population with common features of some kind.

[71] Y. Krishan, "Collective Karmas," *East and West*, December 1989, Vol. 39, No. 1/4, 188.

[72] Entanglement, aka non-locality, is a state in which two or more particles have a cause-and-effect correlation even if separated by large distances.